Curtis Arnold's
PPS
TRADING
SYSTEM

**A Proven Method for
Consistently Beating the Market**

Curtis M. Arnold

IRWIN
Professional Publishing®
Burr Ridge, Illinois
New York, New York

ISBN 1-55738-877-6

Printed in the United States of America

BB

CTV/LH/BJS

1 2 3 4 5 6 7 8 9 0

Table of Contents

```
┌─────────────────────────────────────────────────────────┐
│                      SECTION ONE                          │
│      Laying the Groundwork for Your Trading Success       │
└─────────────────────────────────────────────────────────┘
```

SECTION TWO
PPS Fast Start—Beginners Start Here

SECTION THREE
Deeper into Pattern Research

SECTION FOUR
Additional Technical and
Psychological Considerations

SECTION FIVE
PPS Software and Portfolio Analyzer

List of Figures

List of Tables

Introduction

This book was written to give you the opportunity to join an elite group: a small percentage of traders who make money year after year trading futures. Note: I stated that this book will give you the *opportunity*. That doesn't mean it will be easy. Trading futures or, more importantly, trading futures *profitably* is one of the most difficult tasks you will ever undertake. Any success you achieve will be hard-earned. Sure, it is easy to get lucky; a few winning trades early may make you believe you have the Midas touch. But beginner's luck never lasts long. And if your hope is to make a significant amount of money—and keep it—you will soon see that serious effort on your part is required.

But you do have one advantage. You hold in your hands, not just a book, but *experience*. By carefully following the principles in this book, you can slash your learning curve, start making money right away, and keep on making it. In my nearly 20 years in the futures industry, I've met very few traders who have become consistently successful in less than 10 years. When I started trading in the 1970s, I experienced beginner's luck and concluded that futures trading was easy. After trading successfully for one week, I quit my job as a systems analyst to become a full-time commodity trader. Boy, was I naive!

My beginner's luck soon ran out. Fortunately, however, my knowledge of commodities and my computer background landed me a job at a money management firm. Starting as a technical analyst, I soon advanced to director of the technical research department and was able to hire a staff, including chartists and programmers, to research the many trading techniques and approaches I encountered. My productivity as a research analyst increased dramatically, and from the late 70s through the mid-80s, my research was on the cutting edge. Advances in technical analysis were happening at lightning speed in tandem with advances in the personal computer. During this period, I contributed a fair amount of original research to the field by way of published articles and symposiums. It was also during this time that I wrote the first edition of what later became the widely read *Timing the Market* (Chicago: Probus, 1984).

My purpose here is not to bore you with a biography, but to point out that despite all the resources at my disposal, after an entire decade of full-time research and trading, I was *still* not a successful trader. Did I make money? Overall, yes, but with great inconsistency.

In those days, system traders were a small minority. Most traders were technical analysts, armed only with chartbooks and pencils or with personal computer software that produced a myriad of indicators. The average trader would come up with his own mix, but judgment still played a large role for most traders. Unfortunately, because the judgment factor is a constantly changing variable, when results turn sour it is difficult to know what part of the trading approach is to blame. Changes invariably follow. But since the trader cannot know for certain what part of his trading scheme is at fault, he may change the wrong variable. This never-ending process leads to inconsistent trading results.

I was not able to achieve consistent trading results until I created the PPS Method in 1987. Like so many worthwhile discoveries, I stumbled on to what later developed into PPS quite by accident. Before plunging ahead, however, I'd like to preview where this book will take you.

The book is divided into five sections and appendices; it works best if each section is read in order because it progresses from concepts to details and builds upon the knowledge you gain as you go along. Section One is entitled "Laying the Groundwork for Your Trading Success." I begin with a short background piece about how the PPS system came into being. In the next two chapters, I discuss why most traders lose and what you must do to become successful. You will gain insights into your trading that will break you of bad habits and give you a totally new perspective on your trading; you will need this new perspective to completely appreciate and embrace the PPS approach. The final chapter in this section discusses computerized trading systems in general. I find that newer traders, in particular, have difficulty in separating the wheat from the chaff in this area, and thus have a tendency to fall victim to false claims. I have talked to hundreds of traders who have wasted tens of thousands of dollars because they lacked an understanding of how computerized trading systems are designed. My intent is save you from that fate.

In Section Two, "PPS Fast Start," you will learn a modified version of PPS, designed for the beginning trader. Known as PPS Fast Start, the method is actually a subset of the full PPS Method. It trades fewer markets and takes fewer signals, thereby lending itself not only to the new trader but also the undercapitalized trader. You will have the opportunity to apply what you have learned to actual charts in a practice session at the end of this section.

In Section Three, "Deeper into Pattern Research," you will learn additional entries that will allow you to trade more aggressively. When you finish this section you will command a thorough knowledge of classical chart patterns, based on never-before-published original research. Be forewarned—this particular section is not light reading. If you become bogged down, skip directly to the last chapter of the section, "Building the System." You can always go back later and review the research on the individual patterns at another time. Once again, you will have the opportunity to apply your newfound knowledge to charts at the end of this section.

Section Four examines "Additional Technical and Psychological Considerations." The technical considerations you will learn are understood by less than 1 percent of the trading public. You'll have a definite edge when you have learned how to interpret and forecast price behavior based on a knowledge of commitment-of-traders data, the effect of first notice day and option expirations, and the implications of basis and spread relationships. But technical knowledge is only half the battle; your ability to overcome mental hurdles, the subject of the final chapter in this section, will, in the final analysis, determine your success. There are many good books on personal trading psychology, and this short chapter, mostly written from my own personal experience, should only be considered an introduction. However, it is invaluable to one who wishes to pursue a PPS approach because it is PPS specific. By that, I mean that each type of trading system you encounter will challenge you in a unique way, and the advice given here is designed to help you overcome the mental hurdles unique to PPS.

If you do not own a personal computer, you will have learned everything you need to know to trade the PPS Method successfully after completing the first four sections of this book. If you do use a personal computer in your trading, you may be fascinated by Section Five, where you will learn how the method evolved into a computerized trading system in 1992 (PPS Software), and how, in 1994, a subsequent research program (PPS Portfolio Analyzer) allowed us to apply more intelligent portfolio selection and money management techniques to the method.

Appendices A and B show test results of the original methodology, first comparing performance by sector and then by individual market. Appendix C instructs you how to load and run your PPS Demo Disk.

That's it. I hope you will find the journey exciting. I've done my part; the rest is up to you. So, turn the page and let's get started!

Laying the Groundwork for Your Trading Success

In Section 1, you will gain a foundation of knowledge that will allow you to fully comprehend the PPS Trading System. First you must understand the system's genesis: A brief history will set the stage. But before furthering your knowledge of PPS, certain basics must be mastered. The next two chapters are devoted to teaching you why most traders lose, and what you must do to win. Finally, because PPS is a trading system, you must acquire a degree of knowledge about trading systems. Only then will you be prepared to learn PPS.

The History of PPS

PPS is an abbreviation for Pattern Probability Strategy, a futures trading methodology developed in 1987. As the name implies, the approach employs chart patterns—classical chart patterns whose probabilities of success have been quantified for the first time ever. You'll learn that PPS evolved quite by accident, the result of a research project designed simply to corroborate or refute theories on market behavior espoused by Edwards and Magee in their classic text Technical Analysis of Stock Trends.

I have always been fascinated by price charts. In the 1970s, my office walls were papered floor to ceiling with Gann charts, carefully constructed by hand, 1 by 1s and 2 by 1s—major Gann angles—launched from every major high and low, and lines guaranteed to stop the market cold, banding horizontally like the rings of Saturn. A few years later, I redecorated. Elliott Wave charts now spanned the walls, their unbroken lines zigging and zagging according to what I believed must be some preordained cosmic law. Again, horizontal lines, these based on "Fibonacci" numbers, stratified the chart.

Yet despite my intense interest in these more exotic charts, "real charts"—bar charts, for both stocks and commodities—dominated my work area as soon as the empty cereal bowl was pushed aside and the coffee spill was blotted dry. Of course, like any good technician of the day, my tattered and well-marked copy of Edwards and Magee's *Technical Analysis of Stock Trends* was always within reach, as were copies of books by other chart-oriented technicians whose work actually predated Edwards and Magee's.

As the 80s dawned and I wrote my first book on technical analysis—a text weighted heavily toward stock market analysis—I liberally borrowed the ideas of Edwards and Magee when compiling chapters on chart analysis. After my book, more and more books were published in the field of technical analysis. Reading these books, I became aware that practically all references to charting and chart patterns were verbatim from Edwards and Magee. The fact is that modern-day authors, when referencing classical chart patterns and their predictive value, have done nothing more than regurgitate conclusions set forth by Edwards and Magee. Little, if any, *original* research has been published in this field in nearly 50 years. The implication is that a whole generation of futures traders is trading based on research that *may no longer be relevant*—or, perhaps, never was.

That's right. Maybe it never was. *Futures traders* are making decisions in *futures markets* based on research from a book titled, *Technical Analysis of Stock Trends.* The truth is that Edwards and Magee conducted their research exclusively on *stock* charts, not *commodity* charts. Having traded both types of instruments for many years, I can categorically state that commodities do not behave like stocks. Edwards and Magee knew this also, never intending for their research to be used by commodity traders. I quote from page 175 of their book: "It is not the purpose of this book to explain the operation of commodity futures markets, nor to offer instruction to those who wish to trade therein."

They also cited "intrinsic differences" between stocks and commodities and claimed that some chart formations are "far less reliable" in commodity markets. Possibly unaware of Edward and Magee's caveats, countless traders have with abandon applied advice intended for stock trading to commodity trading. Good God, no wonder so many people have lost money! The time had come to seek the truth.

My challenge lay before me. My goal was to write a new book, an Edwards and Magee type of book, that would examine the implications and limitations of classical chart formations when applied to futures markets. As marvelous as Edwards and Magee's work was, I wanted to be more precise and scientific. No generalities; strict definitions were needed to determine success or failure. Patterns would have to be quantified mathematically—no eyeballing. Stops and exits must be precisely defined. Yes, that was what I would do.

A giant ball descended in Times Square amidst streams of confetti and a cacophonous sea of humanity screaming at the top of their lungs. Dick Clark, one finger tightly pressing an earphone to his ear, held a microphone with the other hand and announced the arrival of 1987. In two days I would sit down at the kitchen table and begin a manual examination of 1,400 commodity charts, 780,000 days in all, 10 years, 30 different markets. I had little money, no job, a sizable mortgage payment, and a wife (now ex-wife) who thought I must be out of my mind.

Each day was the same. My wife would go off to work, and I would sit at the kitchen table for six to eight hours poring over charts. Days turned into weeks, and weeks turned into months. Money grew low, and I took out a second mortgage on the house. Friends and family became increasingly worried about me.

While I don't wish to belabor the point, the fact that I have often "followed the beat of a different drummer" may have worked to my advantage in research and commodity trading, and eventually led to my success. I mention this because you may also feel that you are on a strange and mysterious path, and that you may in some way be breaking from your own past; familiar handholds and support systems may soon slip away. But you can't turn back, or you *won't* turn back, because something ill-defined but powerful is pulling you forward, beckoning you toward what could be a richer and more rewarding lifestyle.

For you, I offer not only the story of PPS, but the story of Curtis Arnold, in many ways one and the same. I hope that, by example, my story will offer you *hope*. Because I had no idea that the same ill-defined but powerful force would lead me to the financial success and independence that I now enjoy.

Now that you know how it all began, it's time to get back to the research. Just what did I learn?

Early Observations from the Research

After months of research, evidence piled up to support my original hypothesis: Classical chart patterns, in themselves, have little predictive value. Why did some patterns work perfectly some of the time but not at all on other occasions? Finally, it dawned on me. I was studying each pattern as if it existed in a vacuum. It was only when I placed a pattern in a market scenario or in a particular market structure that the pattern delivered consistent results. For example, even distinguishing between each pattern's performance in an uptrend versus a downtrend provided astonishing differences.

Oddly enough, Edwards and Magee explained uptrends and downtrends as mirror images. To them, the implications of an ascending triangle in an uptrend were identical to those of a descending triangle in a downtrend. My research proved that this is certainly not true in commodities. A significant difference exists between the two: The ascending triangle produces a far higher probability of success than the descending triangle. Why? In commodities, uptrends and downtrends exhibit distinctly different behavior characteristics, as do the patterns within them. (These behavior characteristics derive from price pressures unique to the futures markets—a result of trading behaviors of speculators and commercials—a topic that will be discussed in a later chapter.)

The answer—why patterns sometimes work and sometimes don't—became evident while isolating those market scenarios that must exist before a pattern can be expected to exhibit a high probability of success. Specifically, the patterns were required to exist within the context of an existing trend. One can think of price movement in these basic terms: First, when looking at a chart, it is easy to observe whether a market is trending or meandering sideways. Focusing only upon those markets that are trending, it is again evident that price progress unfolds as a series of "thrusts" intermittently interrupted by "chart patterns." Those chart patterns may be labeled "continuation patterns," after the fact, if the market embarks upon another thrust. However, if the trend ends, the chart pattern (again in hindsight) is labeled a "reversal pattern."

Because the research indicated that only when placed within the context of a trend did these classical chart patterns offer predictive value, I next implemented trend filters (simple moving averages) to discriminate between those patterns that occurred within well-defined trends and those that did not. At this stage of the research, I was hoping that I would be able to 1) identify a trending market, 2) isolate and identify continuation patterns that would be predictive of further price progress, and 3) isolate and identify reversal patterns that would predict the end of a trend and a price move in the opposite direction.

At this juncture, the methodology became crucial. In the study of patterns, how does one define success or failure? This required me, the researcher, to make a value judgment. In order for patterns to be useful in actual trading, success and failure must be strictly defined. The pattern breakout became the obvious entry point, but what next? I then had to define initial stops; just as in real trading, I could not assume an unlimited amount of risk in hopes the pattern would eventually work. Finally, assuming the trade did progress favorably, I had to determine when to label it a success.

As an experienced commodity trader, I believe that risks must always be kept to a minimum. So, in defining the initial stops, I required that the pattern entry technique be accompanied by a fixed amount or a mechanically based, low-risk initial stop. If, after the pattern breakout, that stop was hit, the pattern was deemed a failure, regardless of future market movement.

When is the pattern-based trade a success? A simple answer is when the trade is exited and there is a profit. But *how* do we exit the trade? I was forced to design rules that would move the initial stop to breakeven upon a given set of conditions and, further, to design rules that would trail the stop as prices progressed favorably. Outside of my awareness, as a result of the steps I was taking in order to effectively evaluate the utility of classical chart patterns, a trading system was evolving.

For every type of pattern and every trade, I computed the points gained or lost. I then determined probabilities of success, as well as risk/reward ratios. Those patterns that rated high on both scales I eventually selected to become part of Pattern Probability Strategy (PPS). But that was still a long way off.

Well into 1987, I was still intent on compiling these statistics and publishing my research in a book—that is, until the research findings became ever-more exciting. Some of the patterns, when implemented within the context of my restrictions, showed extremely high probabilities of success and, even more importantly, very high risk/reward ratios. I decided to take some of the more reliable patterns and back-test them for 10 years over a diversified group of 18 commodity markets. The results were almost beyond belief. With a $25,000 hypothetical account, trading single contracts, the fledgling system never made less than 100 percent per year—and some years the profits were as high as 200 percent! I couldn't believe it. Could this possibly be true? Maybe I had made mistakes in the analysis. There was only one way to find out for sure: I would open a test account. The book could wait.

A System Evolves

In January of 1988, I opened my account and began to trade based on these patterns. When the year was over, my account was up 203 percent with a worst drawdown of 7 percent. Word leaked out, and I was influenced to start sharing my approach. In 1989, I began training students, and by year-end approximately 100 traders had learned Pattern Probability Strategy. I finished the year with my account posting results almost identical to those in 1988, this time up 201 percent. My account now up 900 percent in only two years, I switched to a less aggressive, fixed-fractional approach, but my account continued to increase substantially each year thereafter. By the end of 1991, over 300 students had been trained in the methodology. The following year, one of my students went on to become the number one rated CTA in the country; another won the United States Investing Championship with a return of 216 percent.

1992 was a landmark year for PPS. In January, PPS Software was released. Now, PPS traders could historically test the system and even customize it to fit their needs. Within a year, PPS Software was ranked as the number one trading system in the world by Futures Truth Inc., showing a return of 168 percent. In late 1994, another advance was achieved with the release of the PPS Portfolio Analyzer. With this graphical, Windows-based program, PPS could now be used by any trader in the world to trade any market or combination of markets based on predetermined risk tolerances. An abridged version of this software is included with this book.

My journey began in the 1970s when I read the classic Jesse Livermore tale, *Reminiscences of a Stock Operator*. That slim volume spoke to me and ignited a passion to beat the markets. The journey was much longer and harder than I had ever anticipated. But when the rewards came, they came quickly, and now I have achieved what I wanted from the markets. They gave me the opportunity to create my own destiny. Eventually, they provided me with financial independence. Your journey is beginning now. The book which began in 1987 is finally written. With the knowledge you will gain from it, your journey may be a shorter one than mine.

But before you begin to learn the specifics of the PPS approach, "preschool" is required. You must first accept the fact that most commodity traders never become successful, and you need to understand why this is the case. In the next chapter, you will learn how to avoid seven common traps that ensnare beginning traders.

Chapter 2

Why Traders Lose

> *Make no mistake about it, the vast majority of individual traders who become involved in futures lose money. There is much to learn before one can hope to become successful. Unfortunately, futures trading is one endeavor where mistakes cost money. Typically, the first few years of a trader's career are characterized by a series of misguided efforts—forays into one of the following traps: 1) the option trap, 2) the high commission trap, 3) the guru trap, 4) the high-tech trap, 5) the day trading trap, 6) the small account trap, or 7) the "grass is always greener" trap.*

The Option Trap

It is very unfortunate that many are first exposed to the world of commodity trading by way of options. I say *unfortunate* because buying outright options is a losing game. Every year, thousands of people get stung by commodity options, never to return to futures trading. They leave the markets thinking that commodities is a "crooked" game and tell their friends and neighbors of their bad experience. Because of the stories they've heard, all are then likely to shun anything having to do with commodities.

Although regulatory bodies police the industry, a seedy subset of brokerage houses that prey on uninformed investors still flourishes. These brokerage operations are sometimes referred to as boiler rooms. They are often staffed by young, unscrupulous salesmen; I have never met one who had the faintest idea of how to trade commodities, nor have I ever met one who *cared*. They are salesmen, pure and simple. They make hundreds of cold calls every day, until they reach someone who is uninformed, a little bit greedy, and gullible.

These brokers read from standardized sales scripts that may vary from week to week depending on what commodity is making the news at the time. For example, in my town during the Gulf War, one boiler room was making a fortune selling call options on crude oil to people who had never before traded commodities. It was easy for the brokers to get these people excited about the prospects of higher oil prices.

What the investors did not understand was that before they had the opportunity to buy, prices had already risen substantially. Additionally, the call options were outrageously overpriced due to extreme volatility in the market. It was a classic case of a boom/bust cycle. Only this time, due to the brevity of the conflict, the cycle was compressed. The price of oil plunged as quickly as it had risen, producing losses for the majority of investors who bought late.

Why are uninformed investors attracted to options? Primarily because options are touted as a way to make a lot of money with a small investment and because the investor is also told his loss is limited to the price of the option. Is it true? Do options indeed offer the investor a way to make a lot of money with a small investment? Absolutely—and here are some more ways: Take a thousand dollars, go to the track, and bet on a 40-to-1 long shot to win; go to your local convenience store and buy $1,000 of state lotto tickets; or go to Las Vegas and place the money on a Keno bet. You *can* make a lot of money with a small investment by doing any of these things. But, is it *likely?*

Commodity options lie within the same genre of investments, though they rank near the bottom in expectation of profit. Here's why. With the other gambles, you would attribute your success to luck and squander the winnings on "the good life." However, if you get lucky on your first option trade, the broker will promptly convince you that it was because of his skill; he'll then suggest another trade. The investor who was lucky enough to win the first time out will be drawn back to the game, convinced he can do it again. Eventually, he will lose all his money. It would be just like going back to the racetrack to bet on those 40-to-1 nags every day.

The broker will try to make options sound easy. However, nothing could be further from the truth. Options are extremely complicated instruments that require sophisticated computer models to analyze and a knowledge of statistics to understand. The broker selling you the options does not understand any of this. What he *does* understand is that he wants to sell you the long shots because the far out-of-the-money options are cheaply priced. Because this broker makes a sizeable commission on each one that he sells, the more option contracts you can afford to buy, the more money he will make.

I hope that any time you hear the word *option* you will think twice, unless you have a very thorough knowledge of the subject. Now, let's see what other wrong turns you might take that could cost you dearly.

The High-Commission Trap

Some investors who have traded stocks for years at major firms like Merrill Lynch, Prudential-Bache, Shearson, Dean Witter, and others will hear about futures at a cocktail party or on the golf course, then call their stock broker the next day to get his opinion. If the stock broker is registered to handle futures, he may oblige him. If not, he may refer him to someone else in the firm who is. Either way, the investor may find he is paying a very high commission for the personalized service of the full-service broker. Because futures commissions are quite a bit lower than stocks, this might not be readily apparent.

The unwitting investor now has two strikes against him: 1) a commission rate that is too high, and 2) bad advice. It is almost impossible to be successful in the futures markets if you pay higher than a $50 commission. If you are an experienced trader, you should pay no more than the minimum discount commission you can find where service is acceptable. If you are inexperienced or require certain services that a full-service broker can provide—such as monitoring your trading system intraday—you will need to pay extra.

Are you ready to make your own trading decisions? Think of it this way. No one ever became successful in this business *without* making his own trading decisions. The reason is that you must make mistakes in order to learn. If you let someone else make the mistakes for you, you will eventually have to start at square one. That brings us back to the full-service broker. If you are not able to make your own decisions, you will have no choice but to ask for his advice. And, in all likelihood, your broker is not a good trader. If he were, he would not be a broker (salesman). Instead, he would either trade his own account for a living or manage money. So if your broker wants to give you advice about trading, ask to see his own personal account statements for the previous year. If he can't make money for himself, it's not too likely he'll be able to make money for you.

The Guru Trap

If a trader uses a discount broker and receives advice, not from a broker, but from newsletters and hotlines, he may be in a somewhat better position to make money than the trader who uses the full-service broker. One advantage he has is a lower commission rate. The second advantage is that the advice may be better. That may or may not be the case, however.

A great many novice traders do receive their advice from newsletters. Unfortunately, only a handful of the hundreds of newsletter writers in this business have something worthwhile to say. We will address the issue of following the advice of those few later. First, let's examine the business.

Did you ever wonder who writes commodity newsletters and why? As to who, it is usually someone who has a great interest in the markets but who has never been successful at trading. As to why, generally it gives this person a legitimate reason to stay involved with the markets while providing him a living as well. I personally knew a prominent "advisor"—with over 10,000 subscribers to his newsletter—who never traded commodities himself. Why? Because his trading efforts were not successful. He did make big money, however, advising others what to buy and sell.

"But he *must* have made his subscribers money," you argue, "or he couldn't have stayed in business." Wrong. He never made his subscribers money. He stayed in business because he was an excellent promoter and constantly attracted *new* subscribers. So before you put much credence in one of the guru types because of his "reputation," remember that it may have been fabricated by a public relations firm.

What about following the advice of those few advisors who *do* have something worthwhile to say? It is still unlikely that attempting to follow their advice will make you rich. Several problems arise. First, the average investor typically subscribes to two or three advisory services. He mistakenly assumes that by comparing the recommendations of more than one advisor, he will be able to ferret out and take only the best trades when *all* his gurus agree. This approach totally defeats the purpose.

The second problem is that, even when an investor is loyal to one advisor, he may quickly become discouraged after a series of losing trades and look to follow someone else who is "hot." This becomes a never-ending search.

A third problem is that the guru's advice may be unclear. Advisors typically like to hedge their bets so they can appear to be right no matter *what* happens. Here's a typical line used by one advisor I knew: "The market should head lower punctuated by sharp rallies." If you read that, would you know whether to buy or sell next week? Can you guess how the subsequent issue would begin? Guaranteed to begin in only one of two ways. Either, "In our last issue we successfully predicted the market's current decline..." or, "In our last issue we warned investors to be on the lookout for a sharp rally which is now occurring."

Suppose the advisor is more specific and offers a hot line. The burden then rests on the subscriber's shoulders to: 1) call that hot line every day, thrice weekly, or whatever, for the entire year, and 2) to take every trade advised on the hot line. The typical investor will not do that. Instead, he will impose some filter of his own and skip some of the trades.

Once an investor tires of the frustrations of following a guru, he may then read some books on the market or attend a few seminars. With a bit of technical knowledge under his belt, he then begins to make his own decisions. He is to be congratulated! He has taken the first step on a road that might someday lead to profits. But, of course, it is not that easy. Where is he next most likely to go astray?

The High-Tech Trap

In the 1990s, due to sharp gains in computer processing power and sharp declines in hardware prices, the personal computer became prevalent among most professionals. The typical new trader is likely to own a personal computer and is computer literate.

Because inexpensive charting and technical analysis packages are readily available to the new trader, he will likely employ them in his approach to beat the markets. But once into this mind-set, it becomes very easy to forget the basics. He forgets that the market consists of only price, volume, and open interest—all other indicators are derivative. Often he will duplicate his efforts—viewing five indicators where one would do. The primary problem with this multiple indicator approach is that it promotes confusion: There are always contradictory indicators, so he can always justify his position.

The Day-Trading Trap

Day trading is another siren's song that most often lures the trader to ruin. The attraction of day trading is that the trader feels more in control. He likes the fact that he doesn't have to risk exposure in his positions overnight and can therefore sleep better. The day trader usually requires his own quote machine—a significant expense. Typically his broker will make a lot of money—but *he* won't.

There are several problems with day trading. Commissions and slippage are the first. Combined, they eat up a large percentage of the profit. The second problem is that the day trader's primary competition is the floor trader, and the floor trader usually wins. The third problem is burnout—sometimes six hours in front of a quote screen can seem like a long day. But the most overlooked disadvantage is that the day trader is not able to take advantage of pyramiding techniques that would allow him to make big money when fundamental trends occur.

The Small-Account Trap

Pretend that you want to start a small business. You have a good idea that you think will work. You realize you won't make money overnight; even the best businesses generally take a couple of years of hard work before they start turning a profit for their owners. In the meantime, you have a great deal of expense: leases, inventory, advertising, payroll, and so on. Ask the Small Business Administration what is the primary cause of failure with new businesses. They won't hesitate to tell you it is undercapitalization. Often, a new business owner will have a good idea and work hard to make a success of the business, but he will run out of money before the business comes to fruition.

An investor would do well to think of his futures trading as a business. Instead, though, he is likely to open an account with a small amount of capital and hope he will get lucky. What he fails to realize is that, by taking such an approach, he virtually *assures* his failure. An interesting study was conducted several years ago by a major futures brokerage firm. Thousands of new accounts were tracked for one year to gauge the effect of capitalization. While I can't remember the exact figures, I do remember that of those accounts opened with $50,000 or more, approximately 80 percent were still trading after one year. Only about half of the $25,000 accounts managed to survive. But most frightening is that accounts opened with $10,000 were nearly nonexistent—only about 10 percent were still open. Obviously the traders with the higher account sizes had no advantage other than capitalization. They were able to withstand drawdowns and continue trading. Traders with smaller accounts were knocked out of the box at the first sign of adversity.

Why stack the odds against you when you begin commodity trading? Thinking that you will "try your hand" at commodity trading is the wrong approach. If you don't think that you are adequately capitalized at this time, paper trade until you have saved up enough to open an adequately capitalized account. Although paper trading will not challenge you in the same way that trading with real money would, it is a worthwhile exercise that will allow you to gain valuable experience with the trading methodology you have chosen.

Another course of action is to find a partner. If you only have $5,000, you would dramatically increase your odds of successs by finding a friend, relative, or investor who would be willing to put in another $5,000. You could also form a limited partnership and sell shares in the partnership at $1,000 each. For example, assume that you, the general partner, could put in $5,000. Then, assume that you could find four friends or family members who could each put in $5,000. You would have a commodity pool valued at $25,000—an adequately capitalized account. Of course, this alternative presupposes that you have a workable plan to make money trading commodities. Ideally, you would want to be able to show your investors a hypothetical track record of how your system would have performed in preceding years.

The "Grass-Is-Always-Greener" Trap

I have spoken with thousands of traders over the last several years, and I'm convinced I know why so few traders are successful: lack of consistency. To be successful over the long term, you must be consistent. Unless you trade with a well-defined methodology, you have very little chance of achieving long-term success. It doesn't matter that you have fancy indicators or even that you are a good technician. It doesn't matter that you have real-time quotes or that you subscribe to every hot newsletter writer and hotline that you can find. You will still fail if you do not follow a consistent approach.

But don't system traders lose money, too? Absolutely! Most do. But there are good reasons why. First of all, a lot of bad systems exist, both homegrown and commercial. Unless you know a great deal about markets and trading system design, it is difficult to distinguish a good one (one that has a high probability of making you money in the future) from a bad one (one that will likely start losing money about the time you get it, eventually winding up in the "system graveyard").

What if you do find a good trading system? The question then becomes: Are you a good system trader? Will you take every signal? Can you ignore your own opinions or the opinions of others and just do what your system tells you to do, day in and day out? What will you do when you experience a drawdown? Most people will bail out at the worst possible time, always in search of something better. That's why even people who purchase good trading systems lose money.

Figure 2–1 depicts how the average trader typically aborts even winning systems at the worst possible time. Starting with System 1, he trades from point A to point B in time, then aborts the system and starts with a new system, System 2, which he trades from point C to point D in time, eventually aborting that system also. With System 3, he experiences a longer period of profitability but eventually aborts that system after a drawdown also. Any of the three systems would have eventually brought him profitability; but, instead, he managed to finish with a seriously drained account.

Figure 2–1 **The Human Nature of**
Investing and Trading

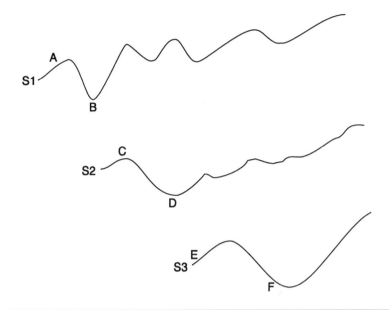

The lesson to be learned is to do your homework before selecting a system. Then, once you've decided on an approach, *stick
with it* through hell and high water.

In this chapter, I have exposed traps that tend to ensnare traders. You should now recognize that 1) options put you at a great
disadvantage, 2) you can not succeed if your commission costs are
too high, 3) you will not find success by following the opinions of
others, 4) technical indicators offer you little advantage, 5) few traders find success by day trading, 6) you are at a great disadvantage if
your account is undercapitalized, and 7) a lack of consistency often
defeats even experienced traders.

Now that you have learned what mistakes to avoid, you are
ready to go on to the next chapter where you will learn exactly
what you *must do* to acquire commodity wealth.

What You Must Do to Acquire Commodity Wealth

The average trader does not view commodity trading as a business—but it is one. Only after you accept the fact that futures trading has more in common with starting a small business than with going to Las Vegas for the weekend, will you have the necessary perspective to make the right decisions in your trading. A small business requires that you invest capital, work long hours, and pay attention to details. If you are successful, you can hope to one day sell the business for a handsome profit and live comfortably from the proceeds. I will show you how it is possible for you to do the same thing in your futures trading business. Are you willing to invest $10,000 today in a business that could be worth in excess of $600,000 in seven years?

Once you have a trading approach (system) that you have confidence in, it is then critical that you start to think long term. Novice traders put too much emotional energy into each trade and overreact to every win and loss. You must learn a new mode of thinking:

Accept the fact that your profits are made over a long series of trades. Therefore, it is counterproductive to worry about whether the trade you put on today will be a winner or a loser.

You must learn to assess risk and reward over time. Focus on the big picture. Where do you hope to be five to seven years from now? Set reasonable goals. Would you be satisfied to make 50 percent per year on your trading capital? That modest goal is not difficult to achieve in the highly leveraged futures markets. It simply means that if you have a $20,000 account, you manage to make $192 each week on average. (In the five years since I began trading PPS, my worst year was 81 percent; my best year was 203 percent.)

To really appreciate the concept of risk and reward over time, study Table 3–1. It becomes clear that "time" is equal in importance to "return" when we consider risk/reward over time. And consistency is the key component of the time element.

Assume that you begin trading with a modest $20,000 account. You have decided that if you lose half, your approach is not viable and you will stop. Therefore, your total risk is $10,000. If you manage to average 50 percent per year in your trading, your account will have grown to $616,944 in only seven years. (A $50,000 account grows to $1,542,360.) Regardless of the size of your account,

---

Table 3–1   **The Power of Compounding**

Investment of $20,000

YEARLY RATES COMPOUNDED MONTHLY

	30%	*40%*	*50%*
Year 1	26,897	29,642	32,641
Year 2	36,174	43,933	53,274
Year 3	48,650	65,115	86,949
Year 4	65,429	96,509	141,909
Year 5	87,995	143,039	231,609
Year 6	118,344	212,002	378,008
Year 7	159,160	314,214	616,944

the risk/reward ratio will have been 61:1. How many investments can you think of today that will be worth 61 times more in seven years—stocks, mutual funds, gold, real estate? Not likely. There is no other investment medium that can offer you the potential to build significant wealth in such a short period of time!

Chapter 4

What You Need to Know about Computerized Trading Systems

Computerized trading systems will dominate futures trading through the remainder of the 90s and into the next century. The majority of professional traders rely to a great degree on some type of computerized trading system. Even amateur traders eventually conclude that a mechanical approach would benefit their trading. But, without a thorough understanding of design factors and performance measures, a computerized trading system can become just one more trap. Before trading a computerized system, you need to kick the tires and look under the hood. What you learn in this chapter will allow you to recognize the misuse of optimization, spot "red flags" that should cause skepticism on your part, and understand basic performance measures that can be applied to any system.

Traders typically progress through stages, initially trading based on news or recommendations from newsletters and hotlines, later progressing to trading based on technical indicators. Finally, they real-

ize that in order to be successful they need to find an objective mechanical system. Having had the opportunity to speak at seminars
to groups of traders at different experience levels, it is quite interesting to observe this phenomenon. Those who are brand new to
trading and flock to the $69 seminars when the show comes to
town want to know one thing: *What are the markets going to do next
week?* The most popular speakers at these events are the ones who
promise to tell them. Mention stochastic indicators or maximum
entropy spectral analysis and their eyes glaze over.

After a year or so, when they have recapitalized their accounts,
they have technical analysis software running on their computers
and 72 different technical studies that draw squiggly lines all over
the charts—and each line can be a *different color!* How can they possibly *not* make money with this much firepower? This group, usually having traded one to three years, crowd into seminars where
the speakers are there to tell them what all the squiggly lines mean.
And, believe me, all those squiggly lines can tell you more than
you need to know. It's almost as though 72 advisors were shouting
out instructions to you at the same time. Who to believe? The loud-
est? Maybe the consensus? It gets quite confusing—but at least
we're having fun! Talk to this group about a simple trading system
that just requires a ruler and charts and they will laugh at you.
Who needs a simple system when we have all these high-tech, ex-
ponentially smoothed oscillators? Traders in this group really still
want to know one thing: *What are the markets going to do next week?*

Usually after about three years or so, when they have once
again recapitalized their accounts, they realize that all their fancy
indicators have failed to make them successful traders. They realize, at last, that in order to be successful *they must follow a system.*
Let the search for the Holy Grail begin!

The first decision you must make is whether to design your
own trading system or to buy one sold commercially. If you wish to
design your own, you can get a programming language that will allow you to do that. Canned routines will make the job easier, and
historical data will give you the ability to test the system once
you've built it. If you're the type that has three or four hours a day
to spend at your computer for the next couple of years, you're in
hog heaven!

However, it has been my experience that those who are attracted early on to this endeavor—the left-brained computer type
who built very large erector set projects as a child—generally lack
the "in-the-trenches" trading experience that is required. They

madly crunch numbers, totally oblivious to what might be points of common knowledge to an experienced trader. When their system is finished, it might look good on paper but it usually won't work in the real world.

Unless you have traded every day with real money for at least five years (preferably 10), your chances of designing a system that is workable in the real world are slim. If you have paid your dues and the word *slippage* has real emotional content for you, you may be ready to design your own system. And, ideally, that is the best route to follow. But, if you can't spare the time, you're going to need to buy a system. Oh lordy, your troubles have just begun.

Buying a trading system is a lot like going to a boat show: Every boat looks so beautiful, majestically perched on its trailer, gleaming in the sun. You buy one and expect it to always look that nice. Maybe they should show you one with barnacles on the bottom, the naugahyde seats cracked, fish guts in the back, and the engine blown. Then you'd know what it would look like in two years. Trading systems are like that.

Here's what you will need to know before you buy a trading system. First, you will need to understand the dangers of optimization. Second, you will need to know the secret techniques that allow system vendors to produce eye-popping hypothetical track records. Third, you will need to recognize red flags that alert you to potential weaknesses of a system. Finally, you will need a basic set of performance measures that will allow you to compare one system to another. If the system vendor refuses to show them to you, buy a boat instead.

Optimization

A simple way to define optimization is this: The system developer has the benefit of hindsight when designing his trading system. Using that definition, all trading systems are optimized to some degree. We must use the past to some degree in order to have a perspective for the future. So optimization, in the simplest sense, is not a bad thing.

The problem with optimization is that at some point a good thing becomes a bad thing. Once the developer has crossed that indefinable, fine line, he can be said to have developed a system that is overoptimized. The designer, with 20/20 hindsight, has adjusted his rules and parameters until his historical results were the best they possibly could have been. "What's wrong with that?" you say.

Another word for overoptimization is *curve fitting*. The tighter you fit your curve to past data, the less likely the future data stream will look the same, and the more likely the future results of your system will be dissimilar to your historical test. In a way, it's a catch-22: You want to use what you have learned about past price history to build your model, but you don't want the model too dependent on that past price history.

The computer makes curve fitting a cinch. You can buy software programs that will allow you to take any set of variables and reiterate through every possible combination of values, ranking them from best to worst in a matter of seconds. I'll never forget the first time I saw the optimization process misused in futures trading. It was in the 1970s when *commodities* was still the prevalent term. Merrill Lynch tested every commodity using every possible combination of dual-moving average crossovers. The computer ranked the performance of thousands of combinations. Then Merrill published the absolute "best" for each market. For example, the best combination for corn might be a 9-day M.A. crossing over a 26-day M.A., while in soybeans, the best might be a 14-day M.A. crossing over a 24-day M.A. You can be certain that their magical combinations were not the best ones to use in the future. Why? Because by selecting the "best" combination, they were overoptimizing or *curve fitting* too tightly to past data.

Unfortunately, most computerized trading systems offered to the public are overoptimized. From a marketing standpoint, the system with the highest return (such as 9,000 percent in the last two years) is going to be bought by more people than one advertised with a 60 percent return. If you had your choice, which would you pick? Even if the first one performed only *half* as well as it did in the past, it would still make you a cool 4,500 percent. Just as unsophisticated individuals will continue to be drawn into futures by the boiler-room brokers selling options, so will others waste their money on overoptimized computerized trading systems.

Creating Eye-Popping Hypothetical Track Records

There are many ways for a system vendor to create systems with fantastic hypothetical track records. In fact, with a little knowledge, you could come up with at least a dozen such systems over a weekend. Here are just two that should serve as apt examples. Let's first build an S&P trading system. We'll design one that only takes long trades, and we'll show a track record from 1982 to 1994. We'll slip in a seasonality factor, so as to keep the system out of the market during the 1987 crash and the minicrash of 1990 as well. We'll take profits every 10 points, so we'll make $5,000 on each winning trade. What about stops? We won't use any. That should assure us of a winning percentage pretty near 100 percent. Now that's an accurate system! Want to buy it?

I hope you said no. But I can assure you that some people would buy the system. You said no because you know something about the market. You know that we were in a bull market during this entire period, and that the system would not perform as well in a bear market. You know that there was a crash in 1987, and wonder why the system wasn't in the market. You know that a system without stops is a recipe for disaster. So, your knowledge of markets protected you from buying an impractical system.

If you think that my hypothetical system was off the wall, I want to tell you a little story. But I won't name names so as to protect the parties involved. There is a rating service that rates computerized trading systems in real time. Just this past year, a particular system zoomed up the charts to number one. The system was designed to trade just one market, one that had been in a bull market for years. A friend of mine, still fairly new to futures markets, showed me a computer run of this system and said, "Isn't this great? Low drawdowns and a high winning percentage of trades. I'm going to trade it."

I asked him for the particulars on the system and found out—are you ready for this?—the system only takes long trades and doesn't use stops. I asked my friend what would happen if a bear market started. Still beaming over the computer run, he must not have heard me. He opened an account for $15,000 and started trading. The bear market began the following week. I watched the market fall and his equity drop. I'd call and say, "Have you gotten out yet?" He'd say, "No, the system says to double up if the drawdown gets this bad." He did. The market continued to plunge, his account went to zero, and he quit. It all lasted about three weeks. This is what can happen if you rely too much on historical track records and don't use common sense.

Ready to build another system? Why not? It will only take a few minutes. We'll pick a few simple variables (we could even use some moving averages, for example). Then we'll run the system on 30 different markets. Since we didn't spend too much time on this system, we can't expect too much. Let's see what we've come up with. Just as I thought, 25 of the markets lost money. But, hey, five out of the 30 actually made money. Now we've got a new system to sell. You guessed it: It was "designed" to trade five markets!

You just learned a couple of ways that system vendors can create eye-popping hypothetical track records. Now I'll show you five "red flags" to look for when shopping for a trading system.

Red Flags

1. **Be suspicious when you see a system designed to trade just one commodity.**

    While this feature alone is not a good enough reason to think that the system will not work in the future, it sure gives you enough reason to investigate the design thoroughly. First of all, these types of systems, by their very nature, are the easiest ones to overoptimize. A designer has far more trouble when he must find rules that worked historically over a wide range of markets.

    Another problem with one-market systems is that any particular market will often change its trading characteristics completely from the recent past. Does silver trade now the way it did a decade ago? How about the oil markets during the Gulf War? You never know when the market you are trading is going to start acting entirely differently. The best way to protect yourself is to use a system that incorporates as much market experience as possible; the best way to do that is to see it perform profitably on a wide range of markets.

    One exception would be if you had a system that was very short-term in nature, such as a day-trading system. Then, in a market such as the S&P, bonds, or a major currency, the system could possibly be validated if you had enough trials in the test period over different kinds of market conditions.

2. **Be suspicious when you see a vendor offering multiple one-market systems for sale.**

    If you bought their T-bond system last year and it did poorly, they'll just shake their heads and say, "I wish you'd had our S&P system—*it* was up over 400 percent." Even more bothersome is that the few organizations that track and rate such systems turn a blind eye to these shenanigans. So, a vendor may have as many as a half dozen such systems. One of them is bound to hit big. It achieves a high ranking

from a rating service, and then this is the one they will pro-
mote—backed up, of course, by objective claims from an im-
partial rating service.

3. **Be suspicious of trading systems with short track
    records.**
    Five years has become a standard and even that may not
    be adequate. I would want to see reasonable consistency
    over a 10-year period. And, again, *consistency* is the key. Tests
    of PPS show nearly identical performance during both the
    first half and the last half of the 1980s. Remember, though,
    that time alone may not be an accurate measure of what we
    are trying to determine. We want to see how the system per-
    formed during differing market conditions. We have to look
    at the price history of the market itself to determine those
    market conditions. For example, 10 years would not be ade-
    quate to test a system if that time period had been a 10-year
    bull market.

4. **Be suspicious of hypothetical track records.**
    Although I have pointed out some of the shortcomings
    of the methods used by organizations that track and rate trad-
    ing systems, their existence has certainly benefited the public
    in many respects. First, systems with only hypothetical track
    records won't show up in the ratings. So, at least if the sys-
    tem you are considering is rated, it has some real-time
    track record behind it. Does a system have to be rated to
    be good? Not at all. Sometimes someone will create a system
    and trade it with their own account to see how well it holds
    up before marketing it. In a case like that, you may be able
    to see the vendor's brokerage statements before buying. An-
    other way to check out a system's real-time performance is to
    ask for references. Then call several people who have been
    trading the system to get their opinions. Sometimes one opin-
    ion may not be enough; different individuals may have to-
    tally different experiences trading the same system.
    Can a system with just a hypothetical track record be any
    good? Absolutely! *Every* system had to start out with only a
    hypothetical track record. The first year I started trading
    PPS, I had only a hypothetical track record to go by. But that
    year I tripled my money. I would have no trouble trading a
    system with only a hypothetical track record if I knew the
    rules—because of my experience in markets and with trad-

ing systems. But for the new practitioner who may lack such skills, finding a system that has *proven* itself in real time is probably the better alternative.

5. **Be suspicious of trading systems in general.**

It would be the exception, rather than the rule, to find in your mailbox an advertisement for a trading system that will make you as rich as it predicts. But, is it possible? Yes. When PPS Software was first released, a small mailing that advertised a hypothetical track record was sent out to prospective customers. One year later, according to the rating services, PPS had actually performed *better* in real time than was advertised in the hypothetical track record.

But, in general it is best to be cautious. There are so many ways I've seen system vendors mislead the public. Here are just a few more things to look out for.

1. They advertise the results of the system without taking into consideration the cost of commission and the inevitable dollars lost to slippage. You should factor in $75–$100 per trade for slippage and commission costs, depending on what markets are being traded. Sometimes an active system will look great—until you factor in these costs.

2. How are the final numbers achieved? If the final equity reflects adding more contracts as the account increases in size (pyramiding), drawdowns could be very large in real dollars and may not represent a practical trading simulation because you would likely have stopped trading before you reached the final figure. It is best to look at two equity curves: one trading only single contracts and another with pyramiding allowed.

3. How is drawdown calculated? I've seen vendors advertise drawdown as a percentage of total profits over a 10-year run. This makes the drawdown look smaller. For example, the system starts with a $25,000 account, and it grows to $525,000 over 10 years. That is not difficult to achieve. But let's assume that the maximum drawdown occurred in the third year, when the account may have gone from $85,000 to $35,000. The drawdown of $50,000 was actually 59 percent. Most traders would have ditched the system after losing

that much. But the vendor advertises the drawdown as "only 10 percent" of profits ($50,000/$500,000).

Basic Performance Measures

One nice feature of computerized trading systems is that they will usually allow you to produce a raft of statistics to analyze the trading system. Just what statistics are useful, and how should you use them? Assume, for example, that the system in question was run over a 10-year period. The first statistic you will look at is the net profit. Divide this figure by the number of years to determine how much the system made on average each year. Look at the variance. In other words, if the system made a lot of money in only three years while in the other years it lost money, this is probably not a system you want to trade. You would like to see it make money *every* year. The more consistent a system, the more it is able to take advantage of compounding of profits, to say nothing of how much more easy it is to trade psychologically.

Also look at the total number of trades. Divide that figure to see how many trades the system takes each month. Is the system too active or inactive for your trading temperament, or is it just about right? Look at the number of winning trades and the number of losing trades, then determine the percentage of winning trades. Beginning traders typically think that a system with a higher percentage of winning trades is better than one with a lower percentage; that may or may not be the case. In order to make a true evaluation, you must also compare the average winning trade to the average losing trade. Systems with a high percentage of winning trades tend to exhibit a lower average win/loss, while successful systems with a low winning percentage will exhibit a higher average win/loss. Either type of system can be very successful.

SECTION TWO

PPS Fast Start—
Beginners Start Here

You are now ready to begin learning the PPS Trading System. In this section, you will learn PPS Fast Start, a modified version of the complete system. If you are new to trading or your account is undercapitalized (less than $20,000), you may wish to trade only this subset of PPS until you gain more experience in the markets.

C h a p t e r   5

PPS Principles

> *In this chapter, you will learn the four tenets of successful
> trading that are the building blocks of PPS.*

The Four Tenets of Successful Trading

1. Trade with the trend.

2. Cut losses short.

3. Let profits run.

4. Use good money management.

In late 1993, I gave a speech to a roomful of traders at the Futures
West conference sponsored by *Futures* magazine. I listed the four
tenets of successful trading, pointing to them on an overhead pro-
jector. I then asked for a show of hands: "How many of you have
heard of these trading rules before?" Nearly everyone raised his
hand. "Now, be honest," I said. "How many of you have followed
those rules consistently throughout the course of the year?" Not
one hand was raised.

"Well, why *haven't* you?" I asked. The question was rhetorical;
I already knew the answer. The reason they weren't able to follow

those rules is because the rules are not specific. They are vague and subject to varying interpretations. What, precisely, does "Let profits run" mean? It might mean one thing to one trader and something entirely different to another. In order to apply the rules, we must make them specific. That is what PPS does.

PPS Fast Start will teach you how to define the trend so you will have no doubt whether you are indeed trading with the trend. It will then give you concise rules that will allow you to place a close initial stop when you enter a trade so that you can cut losses short. Next, you will be given specific rules to trail your stop, allowing you to let profits run. Finally, it will show you how much to risk on each trade so that you can use good money management.

PPS Fast Start makes it easy for you to follow the four tenets of successful trading, because the system was built brick by brick on those proven principles. All you have to do is follow the rules of the system—and you will *automatically* be doing what it takes to trade successfully.

Chapter 6

Defining the Trend

> Trade with the trend *is one of the tenets of successful trading. However, while this is well known, surprisingly few traders adhere to the rule consistently. Many lack a true definition of what constitutes a trend. In this chapter, you will learn a simple definition that will enable you to always recognize when a trend is in effect.*

I cannot overstate the importance of the underlying trend in commodity trading. When asked for trading wisdom, the greatest legendary traders, from Jesse Livermore through Richard Dennis, would simply reply: "The trend is your friend," or "don't fight the tape." And you were expecting something complex and profound? Could commodity trading really be *that* simple? The answer is *yes*. In my opinion, you are halfway home when your trading is based on this simple yet profound truth.

Why Follow Trends?

In commodities, intraday and daily price action is generally the result of "daily" news items and rumors or of orders placed by large traders and floor traders. Price action is *less predictable* and *more ran-*

dom. When viewed over a period of weeks and months, however, this daily price action appears to be nothing more than random noise. Then the true underlying trend becomes quite easily visible. As long-term traders, this is the trend we are interested in. This trend is not influenced by daily news, rumors, or floor traders. Instead, it is the result of fundamental supply and demand imbalances throughout the world in a particular commodity, and it cannot be easily manipulated.

Intermediate versus Long-Term Trends

Trends are of particular importance to anyone who trades with an intermediate or long-term methodology such as PPS. With PPS, each trade is approached with long-term expectations. In reality, most PPS trades are very short-lived and last only a few days. Occasionally, however, we will board a trend that continues for months—and we will make as much as 10,000 dollars per contract on that trade.

You may wonder what determines whether a system is intermediate or long-term. Generally, the exit system makes that determination. In PPS, we could have more multimonth trades—if we were willing to risk a few thousand dollars in open profit each time we were on board a trend. As you will soon find out, PPS is *not* willing to do that. Instead, the exit system is tightly fitted, forcing the market trend to continually prove itself in order for us to stay with the trade. Therefore, an average winning trade may last three weeks, while the longest winning trade rarely exceeds two months.

Conceptualizing the Trend

Imagine a mountain stream, with stepping stones scattered through the stream from one bank to another. Use that analogy to visualize how price patterns and trends interrelate. Price patterns "interrupt" the trend. Just as you need the stones in order to cross the stream safely, you need the price patterns in order to enter the trend safely. The entire PPS system can be seen in those terms: Recognizing the power of trends, the system uses price patterns to allow for safe entry.

Moving Averages

We know the first tenet of successful trading: *Trade with the trend.* But what exactly *is* a trend? Because there are many ways to define a trend, there is no one right answer. All that is important, though, is that we choose one definition, and then trade accordingly: in other words, never initiate a trade unless, by our definition, a trend *does exist.*

Unlike trend lines, which can be subjectively drawn, moving averages are not only a simple way to define the trend, but offer the added benefit of being totally objective. We will use moving averages as trend filters; thus, markets that don't meet our criteria will be eliminated from consideration.

Our first trend filter is the 40-day moving average. Here's how it is applied in PPS:

1. We may only initiate a long position if the 40-day moving average is flat or rising.

2. We may only initiate a short position if the 40-day moving average is flat or falling.

The purpose of this trend filter is to prevent us from initiating positions counter to the major trend. Eliminating this common error will go a long way toward making you a successful trader. The vast majority of small speculators insist upon trying to pick tops and bottoms. This is the wrong way to trade and will lead you to ruin. The legendary investor Bernard Baruch once said that he lets other people have the first third of the move and the last third of the move; he is content with the middle third.

Our second trend filter is the 18-day moving average:

1. We may only initiate a long position if the 18-day moving average is rising.

2. We may only initiate a short position if the 18-day moving average is falling.

The purpose of this trend filter is to ensure that the intermediate-term trend is also in our favor.

By combining both the 40-day and 18-day moving average trend filters, we can be assured that we will not attempt to enter a market unless both the long-term and intermediate-term trends are in our favor.

But what about the short-term trend? Our patterns themselves or, more specifically, the breakout from those patterns, ensure that the short-term trend is also in our favor.

In summary, we now know that we will enter markets only at those optimum times when all three trend components—short, intermediate, and long—are in synch. If you like to think of market movement in cyclical terms, you can visualize three different-length cycle components in synch.

Where can you find these moving averages? If you use a computer, you will find dozens of inexpensive charting programs that will allow you to plot moving averages. If you don't use a computer, many charting services conveniently provide both moving averages on their charts.

Chapter 7

Fast-Start Entries

> *Once you have identified a trend, you must find a way to get on board. In this chapter, you will learn three different patterns and their corresponding entry techniques, which will allow you to enter a trend with a limited risk.*

Excerpted from my original research journal:

November 16, 1987: "The last three months have been spent in an exhaustive attempt to locate, classify, and learn from 118 symmetrical triangles identified over a 10-year period in 30 different commodities. Unlike the double bottoms, the first pattern I researched, results of analysis of symmetrical triangles were startling and should prove to be a basic building block in a comprehensive trading methodology based on chart patterns."

The Symmetrical Triangle

The symmetrical triangle is the core pattern in Pattern Probability Strategy, and the one that you will use most often in PPS Fast Start.

Defining the Pattern

The symmetrical triangle, also referred to as an equilateral triangle, is characterized by four different points: 1) a peak, 2) a retracement, 3) a swing counter to the retracement that falls considerably short of the first peak, and 4) a retracement of that swing that falls considerably short of the first retracement. A trend line drawn connecting points 1 and 3 converges with a trend line drawn connecting points 2 and 4 (see Figure 7–1).

Defining the Signal

Once four distinct points have formed, allowing trend lines to be drawn, a break of the trend line (which signifies a continuation of the previous trend) by one tick intraday constitutes a signal to enter the trade at that point (see Figure 7–2).

Placing the Initial Stop

The point where the two trendlines converge is known as the apex, and a horizontal line drawn through the triangle at the point where the two trendlines converge is the apex line. As soon as you have entered the trade, you should place your stop (assuming you are long) one tick below the apex line. A good time to place your protective stop is when your broker calls you with your fill on your entry. If you place your stop as a day stop, you will need to reenter your stop the following day. I place my stops as "good till canceled" orders. That way, my protective stop is entered automatically every day, and I don't have to worry about it. If you elect

---

Figure 7–1   **Symmetrical Triangle**

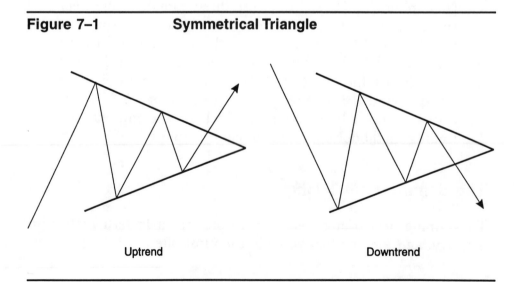

Uptrend   Downtrend

Figure 7–2   **Symmetrical Triangle—Entry**

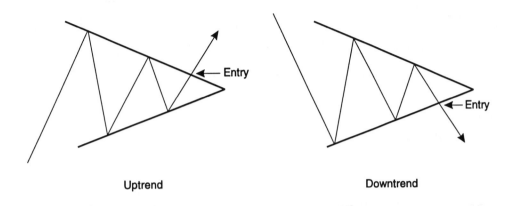

Uptrend   Downtrend

---

this method, you must remember to cancel and replace your order each time you wish to change your stop (see Figure 7–3).

The symmetrical triangle pattern may be used both in uptrends and downtrends.

Size of the Pattern

When I did the original research in 1987, I required the symmetrical triangles to be at least 10 days and no more than 50 days long. In the last few years, however, I have gravitated toward smaller, more compact patterns. By doing so, my stop can be closer. This is an advantage when using a fixed-fractional money management ap-

---

Figure 7–3   **Symmetrical Triangle—Stop**

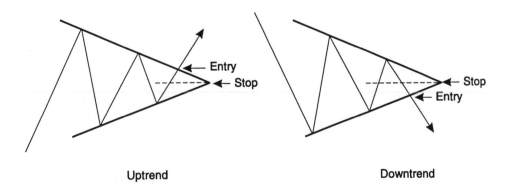

Uptrend   Downtrend

proach (discussed in a later chapter), in that more contracts can be traded. Therefore, you may wish to consider triangles as small as five days long.

When working with smaller triangles, a good rule of thumb is that each swing or leg should be at least two days long. A wide range day would be an exception, in which case one day may comprise a complete leg. To determine whether a new leg has formed, look to see if the previous minor trend, formed by the previous leg, has been broken. If so, you can label a new leg; otherwise, the last leg is still in effect.

Notes from the Research

In commodities, symmetrical triangles overwhelmingly resolve themselves in the direction of the trend. In fact, of the 118 triangles identified, 102, or 86.4 percent, broke out in the direction of the trend. Success is 50 percent more likely if the triangle is only traded in the direction of the trend. Specifically, 37.3 percent of trades were successes with the trend, compared to 25 percent countertrend.

Looking at the percentage of trades that were profitable, 51 percent were profitable in the direction of the trend, while only 31.3 percent were profitable countertrend. Given this information, we can conclude that we should only consider trading those symmetrical triangles that break in the direction of the trend (which, coincidentally, five out of six do) and ignore those triangles that resolve themselves countertrend.

Of 102 trades, 52 were profitable, while 50 either broke even or resulted in losses. Total profits were 2,572 units, or 49.5 per winning trade. Total losses were 210 units, or 4.2 per losing trade. The average trade produced a profit of 23.2 units.

The results are truly astounding! The data are basically telling us that by following this strategy, every other trade will be a winner, and the amount of dollars won in winning trades will average nearly 12 times that lost during losing trades. Of course, loss due to commission and slippage must then be factored in. Factoring in two units per trade, the average trade is still 21.2 units, with winners averaging 47.5 units and losers averaging 6.2 units. Profits are still better than 7:1 with 51 percent of the trades profitable.

To summarize the results:

1. Five out of every six symmetrical triangles resolve in the direction of the trend.

2. Symmetrical triangles should only be traded in the direction of the trend.

3. By limiting losses to a breach of the apex, a very high risk/reward ratio can be achieved while allowing approximately half of all trades to be profitable.

Essentially, the symmetrical triangle creates a low-risk opportunity to establish a position in a trending market whose trend is highly likely to continue.

The Ascending Triangle

The ascending triangle is the second most significant pattern in Pattern Probability Strategy. More rare than the symmetrical triangle, only one-third as many of this pattern was found in the research.

Defining the Pattern

An ascending triangle is bounded by a supply line that is nearly horizontal and a demand line that slants upwards. Like the symmetrical triangle, it is composed of a minimum of four distinct points from which trendlines may be drawn (see Figure 7–4).

Defining the Signal

Once the ascending triangle has formed, a signal is generated when the supply line is breached (upside breakout). Enter the market on a stop placed one tick above the supply line (horizontal line) (see Figure 7–5).

Figure 7–4   **Ascending Triangle**

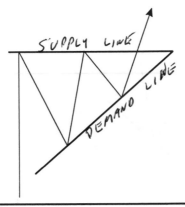

Figure 7–5   **Ascending Triangle—Entry**

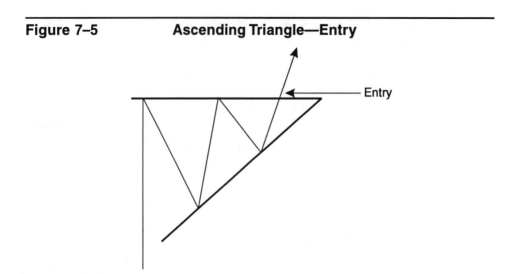

Placing the Initial Stop

A line is drawn that bisects the angle where the supply line and demand line meet. This line is called the *bisected angle.* The initial stop is placed one tick below the bisected angle (see Figure 7–6).

When to Use the Pattern

The ascending triangle entry is used only in uptrends. Fortunately, 93 percent of all ascending triangles are found in uptrends.

Size of the Pattern

Follow the same guidelines as used with the symmetrical triangle.

Figure 7–6   **Ascending Triangle—Stop**

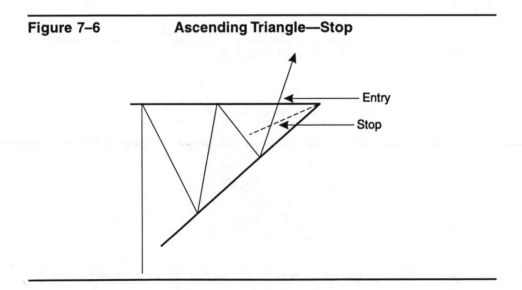

Notes from the Research

Of the 39 ascending triangles traded, 18, or 46 percent, resulted in profitable trades. Defining success as a profit of at least three times the initial risk, the strategy achieved 14 successes. More relevant is the number of units gained on winning trades: 574; the number of units lost on losing trades: 151; and the total net profit: 423 units. We can then find the average win: 31.9 units; the average loss: 7.2 units; and, most importantly, the average units gained per trade: 10.8. All of these numbers should then be reduced by two to account for slippage and commission.

The percentage of winning trades (46 percent) compares relatively well to that of symmetrical triangles (51 percent), but the average net winning trade is far less: 31.9 units compared to 47.5 units. While I cannot offer an explanation for this, the evidence is clear that the post-triangle thrust is generally far weaker in the ascending triangle.

To summarize:

1.   Ascending triangles are only one-third as plentiful as symmetrical triangles.

2   The great majority (93 percent) are found in uptrends.

3.   The ascending triangle entry strategy is profitable, though far less so than the symmetrical triangle entry strategy.

Skewed Triangles

Sometimes you will see a triangle that is skewed—that is, its appearance is between those of a symmetrical triangle and an ascending triangle. The supply line is not horizontal, yet the triangle is not equilateral either. Use a bisected angle for stop placement. If a symmetrical triangle is skewed so that the supply line (top boundary) is flatter than the demand line (bottom boundary), the apex line will cause the stop to be too tight (too close to your entry). If you bisect the angle and place your stop below the bisected angle line, you will have more breathing room and will be less likely to be stopped out by intraday noise.

Further Guidelines

Ascending triangles appear to offer more reliability once the trend is well under way. Look to trade them when found high up in the

trend, and use caution when they are found in an uptrend still in its
embryonic stages.

The Head-and-Shoulders Continuation Pattern

This rare but powerful pattern is not part of the original Pattern
Probability Strategy because its occurrence is so rare that its statistical significance could be questionable. Also, quite frequently, the
right shoulder (uptrend) forms a symmetrical triangle—so the trade
is enacted anyway, without the recognition of the head-and-shoulders continuation pattern.

Defining the Pattern

When in an uptrend, we look for a head-and-shoulders top. The
pattern consists of a head, a left shoulder, and a right shoulder (see
Figure 7–7).

Defining the Signal

Having found the head-and-shoulders top pattern, traditional chart
analysis would dictate shorting the market on a break of the neckline. That would be top picking, however. Instead, we look for a
failure of the pattern: evidence that the underlying trend is so powerful as to negate what would appear to be a topping pattern. That
evidence presents itself when the market, instead of breaking down
once the head-and-shoulders top has completed, moves higher and
exceeds the right shoulder (see Figure 7–8).

Figure 7–7   **Head-and-Shoulders
Continuation Pattern**

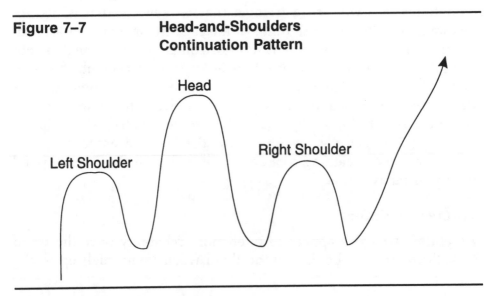

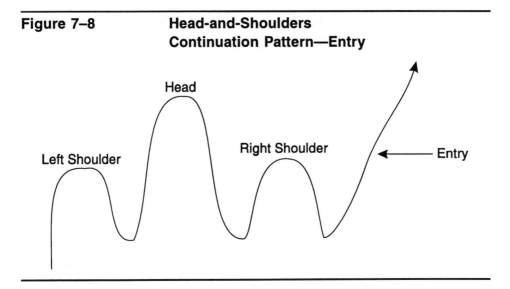

Figure 7–8   **Head-and-Shoulders Continuation Pattern—Entry**

Placing the Initial Stop

Fast-start traders should place the initial stop one-half the distance between the breakout point and the original neckline. If the risk is greater than $400, revert to a $400 money management stop instead (see Figure 7–9).

When to Use the Pattern

If you wish to limit your trading frequency and increase your probability of success on each trade, you should take the right-shoulder trade only in uptrends. In markets such as interest rates and curren-

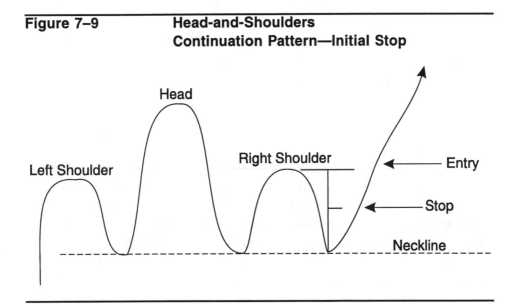

Figure 7–9   **Head-and-Shoulders Continuation Pattern—Initial Stop**

cies, however, there is really no up or down. For instance, long the U.S. dollar is very often a nearly identical position to short the D-mark. Therefore, in those markets, when you are in a downtrend, you should be ready to take short positions on a break below the right shoulder of a "head-and-shoulders bottom."

In downtrends, the break of the right shoulder of a head-and-shoulders bottom is a valid signal in other markets as well. However, because in physical commodities pattern success in general runs higher in uptrends, beginners might consider using the right-shoulder trade only in uptrends. Later, when you have more market knowledge, you can add the right-shoulder head-and-shoulders bottom signal to your arsenal.

Size of the Pattern

The head-and-shoulders patterns will generally be quite a bit larger than the triangles; it takes longer for the left shoulder, head, and right shoulder to form. Ten to 50 days encompass most of the head-and-shoulders patterns you will use.

It is important that your pattern look as similar to a completed head-and-shoulders top as possible. Each of the three components—head, left shoulder, and right shoulder—should form over approximately the same time period. The shoulders should be at approximately the same height. It is all right for the neckline to be sloped slightly up or down. The right shoulder, however, should be fully formed: price must at least approach the price level of neckline. The price may hold slightly above the neckline or break below it by a small amount. Quite frequently, the price will break below the neckline, clear out stops of former longs, sucker in new short sellers, and then come roaring back into the pattern. While it is common for the price to bounce back up to the neckline after hitting these stops, further price movement above the neckline and into the pattern is a show of strength.

How Much to Risk

The mechanical stop based on the signal itself will determine how much you must risk in order to take the trade. However, you must then overlay your own money management system, which will further filter some of the signals you can't afford to take.

It is a misconception that you must risk a lot to make a lot. Remember, in my personal trading account, I risk only one-half of 1 percent of my capital on each trade. How much *you* can afford to risk is based on the size of your account. If your account is between $10,000 and $20,000, you should risk no more than $400 on any trade. Sometimes, you will be able to enter trades where your stop dictates a risk in the $200–$300 range. These are good trades when you can find them. If you get a signal where the risk is greater than $400, it is best to skip the trade. There will always be another trade—but your initial stake is *precious.*

Fast-Start Exits

> *As soon as you enter a trade, you must formulate a definite plan as to how and when you will exit. In this chapter you will learn two rules that will allow you to move your stop to breakeven, thus reducing your risk to zero. After that, you will learn two exit systems—one based on price, the other based on time—that work hand in hand to assure that you lock in open profits as the trend continues.*

The Break-Even Stop

The concept of the break-even stop, as I apply it, is one of the most important trading techniques you will ever learn. As traders, we are at play in a world of ever-changing odds. We must always think in terms of risk/reward and preservation of trading capital. When we enter a position, we enter the arena of risk/reward by defining our risk on the trade. We enter our initial stop at a point that guarantees we will not lose too much of our capital if we are wrong. If we are correct, we cannot determine how much we will make. It may be a little; it may be a lot.

If we examine all our winning and losing trades, we will find an interesting discrepancy: Our losing trades will be in a range of

–$1 to –$400. Our winning trades will be in a range of $1 to $10,000+. Although we will have far more losing trades than winning trades, the average winning trade will be many times larger than the average losing trade.

Since the winning trades will take care of themselves, we need to focus on the losing trades. Here is where we can perform risk/reward magic—the kind of magic that will give us a definite edge in our trading. If we can move our stop to breakeven, we can dramatically shift the risk/reward of any trade in our favor. Our risk is then zero; our reward may be anywhere from $1 to $10,000+. That's my goal on every trade I take!

That's one good reason to get our stop to breakeven. But there is also a technical reason. My research has shown that most of the really big winners (outlying trades) don't hesitate or fool around. They just take off and never look back. If we get a signal and the market doesn't take off within a few days, chances are pretty good that something is wrong and that the trade is going to turn into a loser. By getting our stop to breakeven, we prevent a losing trade. You know how adamant I am about cutting losses. Now we're taking it one step further: wherever possible, cutting our losses to *zero*.

The market is a function of price and time. On a chart, vertical movement of price is represented by the *Y* axis; horizontal movement of time is represented by the *X* axis. We must always take both into consideration when designing our exits. Therefore, we will have two ways to get our stop to breakeven: one based on price movement, the other based on time movement.

Rule #1

Our first rule is: We will move our stop to breakeven as soon as the profit in the trade (based on intraday price movement) is double our initial risk. For example, assume we buy gold at $380 and our stop is at $376. We've risked $4 ($4 * $100 per oz. = $400). As soon as the price reaches $388, or twice our initial $4 risk ($388 – $380 = $8), we move our stop to $380 (breakeven, or the price at which we entered the trade).

Our reasoning? Once the market reaches $388, it should not suddenly turn around and come back to $380. If it does, something is terribly wrong, and the odds are that prices will continue to fall. The market has shown that it now wants to move down, so why wait to get murdered? Let's get out with our skin. Most nonprofessional traders don't think that way. Because they have invested so much emotional energy in the trade, they would rather hold on to even a slim hope that the market will turn back up before hitting their stop. And it just might. But it's not the way to bet (see Figure 8–1).

Rule #2

The second rule addresses the time component of the market. As I stated earlier, my research has shown that if we get a signal, and the market doesn't take off in our direction within a few days, something is wrong. Therefore our second rule is: We will move the stop to breakeven on the fourth day after entry if there is a profit in the trade. If our trade is losing money, we will leave our stop at the original initial stop.

Let's apply this rule to our gold example. Again, assume that we bought gold at $380 and our initial stop is at $376. On the fourth day after entry, the price is $385. The highest price reached since our entry was $386, so we haven't been able to move our stop to breakeven per rule number one. But rule number two, based on time, has now come into play. We move our stop to breakeven, regardless of the fact that our profit is not twice our initial risk (see Figure 8–2).

Again, let's look at the gold example. Assume that on the fourth day after entry, the price is at $378. What do we do? *Nothing.* At this point, it is best to just leave our original stop at $376.

Summary of Break-Even Stop Rules

1. Move your stop to breakeven as soon as the open profit equals twice the initial risk.

2. Move your stop to breakeven on the fourth day after entry if there is a profit in the trade.

Figure 8–1   Break-Even Stops

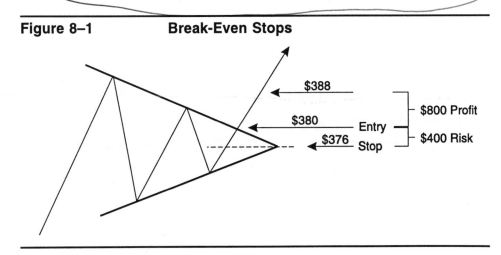

Figure 8–2   **Break-Even Stops**

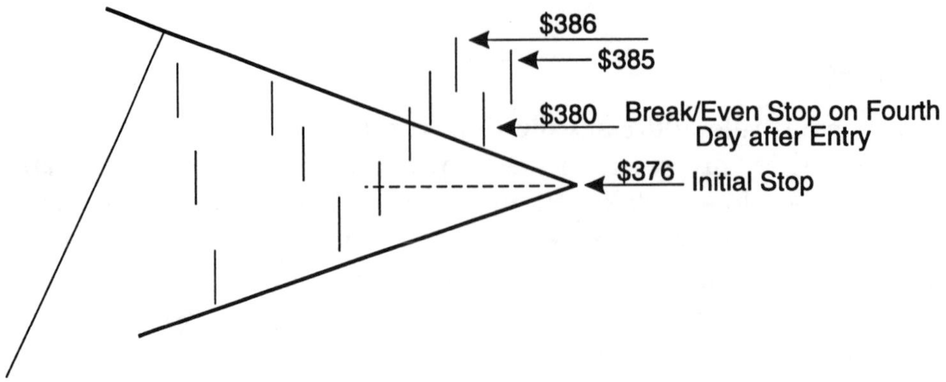

$386

$385

$380   Break/Even Stop on Fourth
              Day after Entry

$376   Initial Stop

Trailing Stops

Once your stop has moved to breakeven and the market continues
to trend in the anticipated direction, your exit system comes into
play. The exit system must conform to the tenet that advises you to
let your profits run; yet it must also be designed so that you will
have some way of locking in profits as they accrue. The fast-start
exit system is actually a combination of two exit systems: one
based on price, one based on time. The two systems may be referred to as the swing supports and the logical trend line.

Swing Supports

Of the two systems, the swing supports will dominate the action 80
percent of the time. In an uptrend, we trail our stops under swing
supports "power of two" (see Figure 8–3). A swing support power
of two assumes that the market, in an uptrend, has pulled back (a
retracement). The low day of that retracement is immediately preceded by two days whose lows are higher than the low of the low
day. Additionally, immediately after the low day are two days
whose lows are also higher than the low of the low day. To summarize, the swing support power of two is a day that is both immediately preceded and followed by two days whose lows are higher
than that day. When a swing support power of two occurs, you
should place your stop one tick below the swing support low.
      Exception: If a wide range day (a day whose range (H-L) is
abnormally large) occurs on the low day or the day subsequent to
it, the low day qualifies as a swing support (see Figure 8–4).

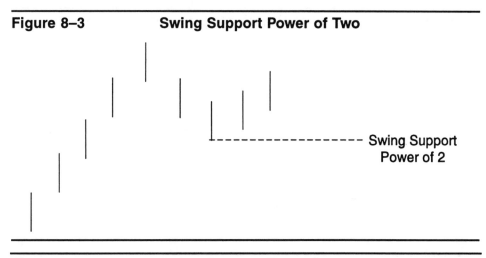

Figure 8–3   **Swing Support Power of Two**

Swing Support Power of 2

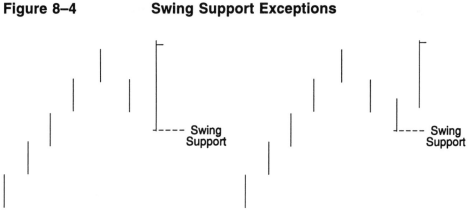

Figure 8–4   **Swing Support Exceptions**

Swing Support

Swing Support

Swing Resistance

When in a downtrend, reverse the process. The swing support then becomes a resistance point. Place your stop one tick above the resistance point power of two (see Figures 8–5 and 8–6).

Logical Trend Line

Sometimes a market will trend without giving you convenient swing supports to trail your stop. In such cases, you may be able to rely on a logical trend line. A logical trend line is one that is drawn under support points as the trend proceeds. The trend line should not be too steep; if you have drawn a very steep trend line on your chart, it is not a logical trend line. There is a good chance it will be broken and, after a slight correction, the market will continue its trend.

Figure 8–5   **Swing Resistance Power of Two**

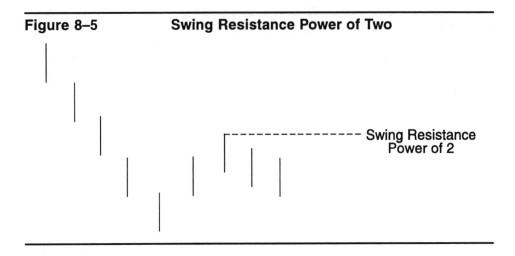

Figure 8–6   **Swing Resistance Exceptions**

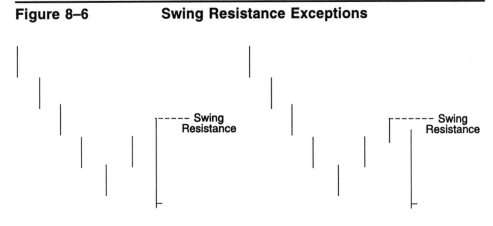

On the other hand, a logical trend line, when broken, often indicates a change of trend. A logical trend line is one that approximates a 45 degree angle on your chart. Place a stop one tick below the logical trend line. Your stop will trail or move higher with the trend line each day (see Figure 8–7).

Important Note: Between the two stops, swing support and logical trend line, use the stop that is tighter; in other words, the one that locks in the most profit on your trade (see Figure 8–8).

Figure 8–7   **Logical Trend Line**

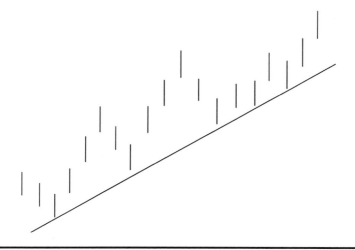

Figure 8–8   **Combining the Two Exit Systems**

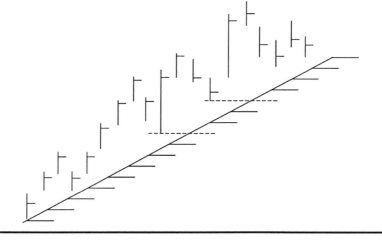

Chapter 9

Fast-Start Portfolio

> *Not all futures markets exhibit similar market behavior; some are more suited to trend—following approaches than others. In this chapter, you will learn which are the better markets to trade with PPS and which should be avoided.*

Pattern Probability Strategy trades 31 markets, including most futures markets with the exception of stock indexes and meats.

Stock indexes are eliminated from consideration for two reasons: First, they are very volatile markets. Attempting to enter a trend with a close stop is not practical. Second, stock indexes are a different animal. Among system designers, they are known as "back-and-fill markets" while all other markets are "break-and-go markets." That means that when stock indexes break out of a pattern or above a resistance area, prices tend to fall back into the pattern rather than continuing in the direction of the breakout.

The meat complex is generally avoided by technically oriented professionals; an examination of open interest highlights this fact. The battle, for the most part, is fought between commercials and small speculators. The few professionals that trade in this complex are usually fundamentally oriented. Whereas most other commodities are global in nature, the meats are a domestic market and, it

has been speculated, subject to manipulation by commercial interests. Regardless, historical testing quickly illustrates the fact that the
meat markets exhibit a "choppiness" much of the time that frus-
trates the technically based trend follower.

Guidelines for the Market Complexes

Assuming you have a small account (under $20,000), portfolio
management is extremely important. You must guard against having too many positions on at one time and, more importantly,
against similar positions in correlated markets (markets that tend to
move together). We'll begin by looking at each market complex,
discussing the vagaries, correlations, and contract sizes of each.

   Copper is a good market in terms of contract size and is not
highly correlated with other markets.

   Gold is a good market. During volatile periods, a Mid-Am contract is available that is one-third the size.

   Platinum is a good market. However, do not trade it in con-
junction with *Gold* as they are highly correlated.

   Palladium is too thin (low liquidity causes slippage) and should
be avoided.

   Silver is a good market but should not be traded with *Gold* or
Platinum.

   T-Bills and *Eurodollars* are good small contracts with plenty of
liquidity. Never trade both together. Of the two, *Eurodollars* are the
better choice because of a greater daily range and better liquidity.

   T-Bonds are a favorite market of all traders because of their
good daily price movement and exceptional liquidity. Even the
Mid-Am contract is liquid and, at one-half the size of the Board of
Trade contract, is a good choice for the small trader.

   Muni-Bonds, T-Notes, and *Five-Year Notes* are all good, liquid
contracts that may be traded in substitution for the *T-Bond* contract.

   The *CRB Index* should be avoided. It will likely only duplicate
your other positions.

   Corn is an ideal market for the small trader, as is *Oats.* Some
correlation exists.

   Soybeans, Soybean Meal, and *Bean Oil* are wonderful markets but,
of course, are highly correlated. Only trade one at a time.

   Rice is too illiquid. Avoid it.

   Canola, traded in Canada, requires a currency conversion.
Avoid it.

Wheat is a good market and not necessarily correlated to the other grains. The *KC Wheat* or *Minn. Wheat* may be traded also.

Cocoa is a good market.

Coffee is a wonderful market that offers spectacular trends.

Sugar is not one of my favorite markets, but may be traded.

Orange Juice, while thin at certain times of the year, offers spectacular trends.

Lumber should be avoided by small account traders. It is very thin, and stop orders are subject to slippage. A greater problem is the market's tendency toward limit moves.

Crude Oil, Heating Oil, and *Unleaded Gas* are great markets. Only be in one at a time. *Natural Gas* is a great market also and is not price correlated to the other three.

Among the currencies, trade *British Pound, Swiss Franc, D-Mark, Japanese Yen, Dollar Index,* and *Canadian Dollar.* Trade only Mid-Am contracts in the SF, DM, and JY. Trade only one market at a time to avoid correlation.

No Meats! No Stock Indexes!

Number of Positions in the Portfolio

At certain times, correlation among *all* markets increases. Examples include times of powerful interest rate expectations or geopolitical upheavals. Therefore, fast-start traders should limit the number of positions in their portfolio at any one time to four.

Chapter 10

Practice Sessions

Following are 23 charts that will give you practice in identifying patterns, drawing trend lines, and placing stops. To simulate real-time trading, cover up the right side of the chart with a piece of paper. Then move the paper to the right, one day at a time. When you have found a pattern, draw it in. Mark where you would enter the trade. Move your stop as you move the paper to the right one day at a time. Draw in a logical trend line if you can find one. Be alert for swing supports (resistance).

You will be asked to perform certain exercises, such as find the triangle, trail the stop, draw a logical trend line, and so on. In addition to performing the exercises, use what you have learned so far to practice your trading. After attempting the first chart, skip forward to the answer section and compare your interpretation to mine. If you had any difficulties, go back and review your chart again. If something is still not clear, you may have to review the rules again. Once you are satisfied that you understand the chart, go on to the next one.

Note: You may wish to remove your practice charts and photocopy them before you mark on them. Another alternative, just as practical, would be to mark in pencil so you can erase any errors.

These 23 charts are just a start. The more you can practice on historical charts, the better you will become at identifying patterns correctly. In addition to increasing your skill, historical paper trading will also build your confidence in the approach. The more confidence you gain, the easier it will be for you to stay with it.

One word of caution before you begin: Many beginners, a bit overzealous, find patterns where none exist. That can be even more of a problem than failing to identify a *real* pattern. So, remember to be discriminating—and follow the rules.

Now, turn the page and get started!

Student's Practice Charts

Figure 10–1

November 1991—Orange Juice

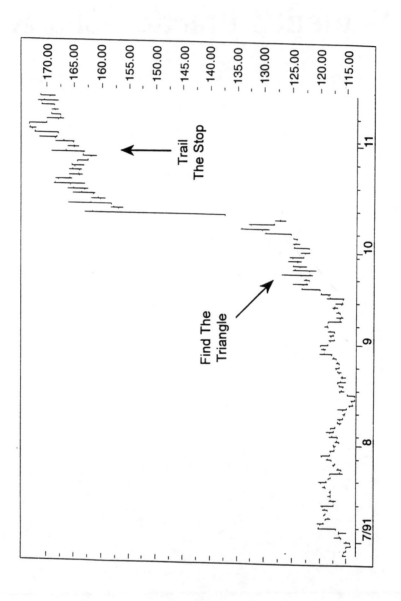

Figure 10–2

January 1988—Soybean Oil

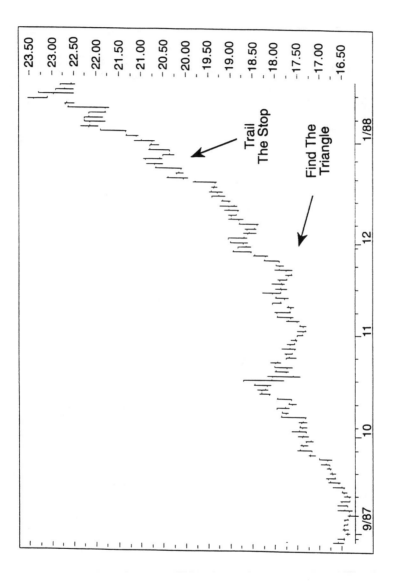

71

Figure 10–3

January 1988—Soybeans

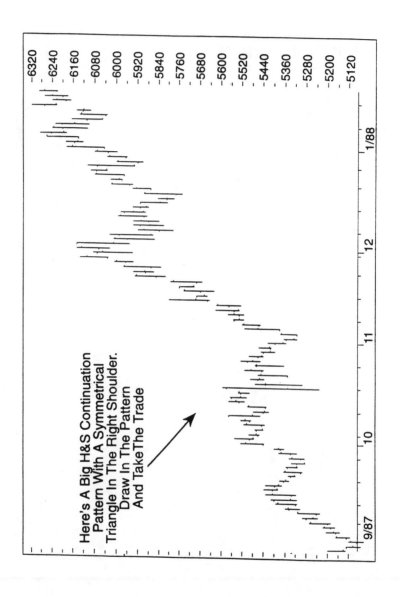

Here's A Big H&S Continuation
Pattern With A Symmetrical
Triangle In The Right Shoulder.
Draw In The Pattern
And Take The Trade

Figure 10–4

July 1993—Lumber

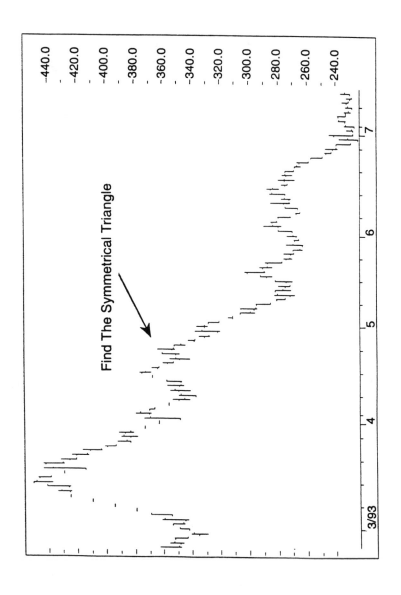

73

Figure 10-5

January 1990—Lumber

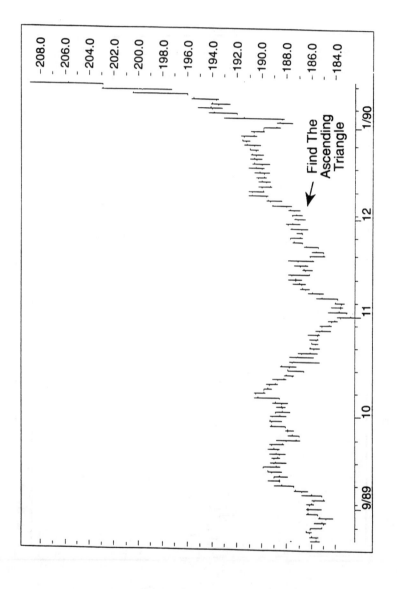

74

Figure 10–6

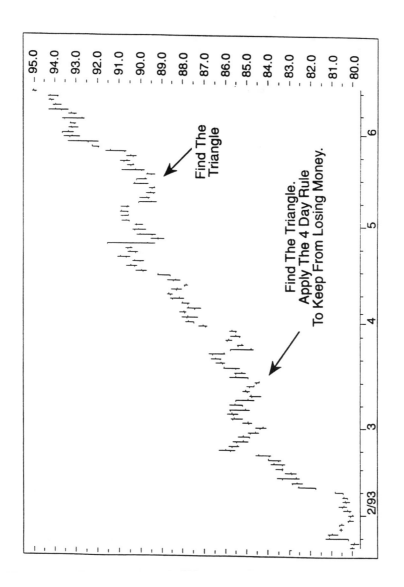

June 1993—Japanese Yen

Figure 10–7

March 1993—Japanese Yen

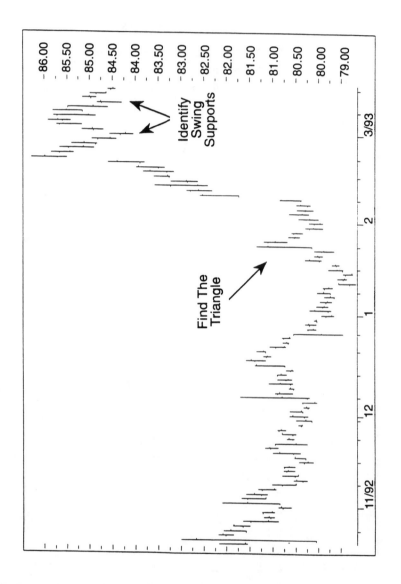

Identify
Swing
Supports

Find The
Triangle

86.00
85.50
85.00
84.50
84.00
83.50
83.00
82.50
82.00
81.50
81.00
80.50
80.00
79.00

11/92   12   1   2   3/93

76

Figure 10-8

December 1991—Japanese Yen

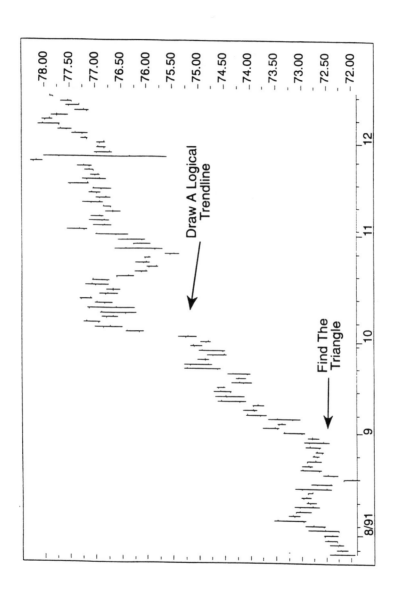

Figure 10–9

March 1988—Japanese Yen

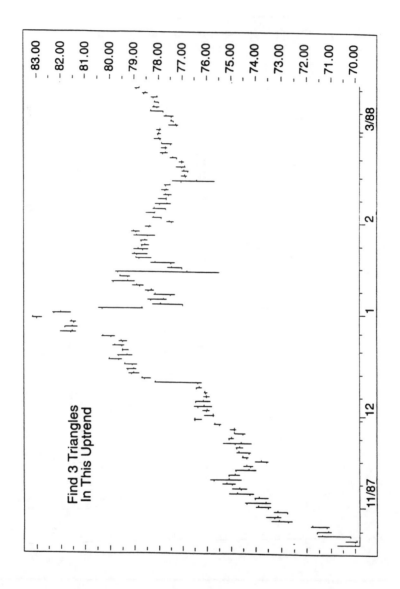

Figure 10–10

December 1982—Coffee 'C'

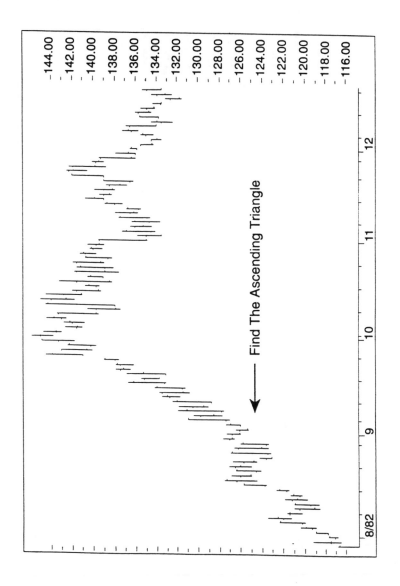

Figure 10–11

December 1985—Coffee 'C'

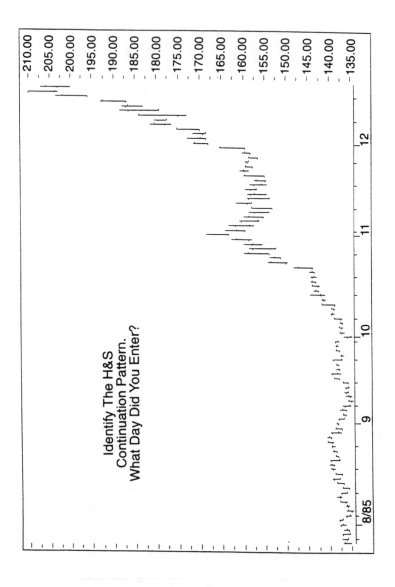

Identify The H&S
Continuation Pattern.
What Day Did You Enter?

80

Figure 10–12

December 1988—Coffee 'C'

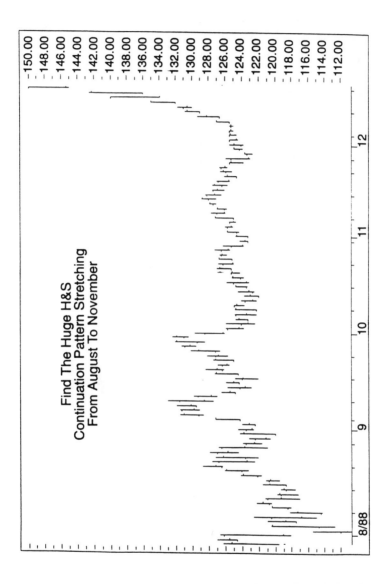

Find The Huge H&S
Continuation Pattern Stretching
From August To November

81

Figure 10–13

March 1974—Sugar #11 (World)

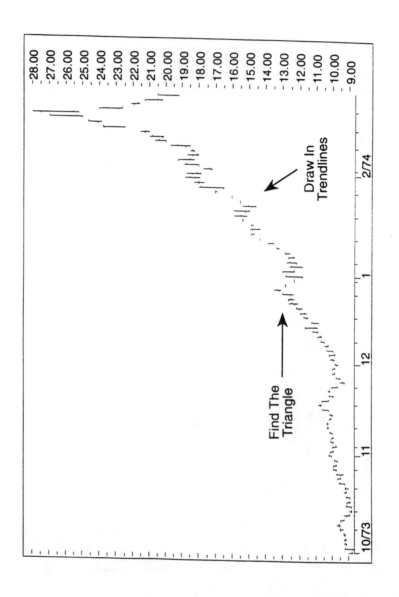

Figure 10–14

September 1984—Sugar #11 (World)

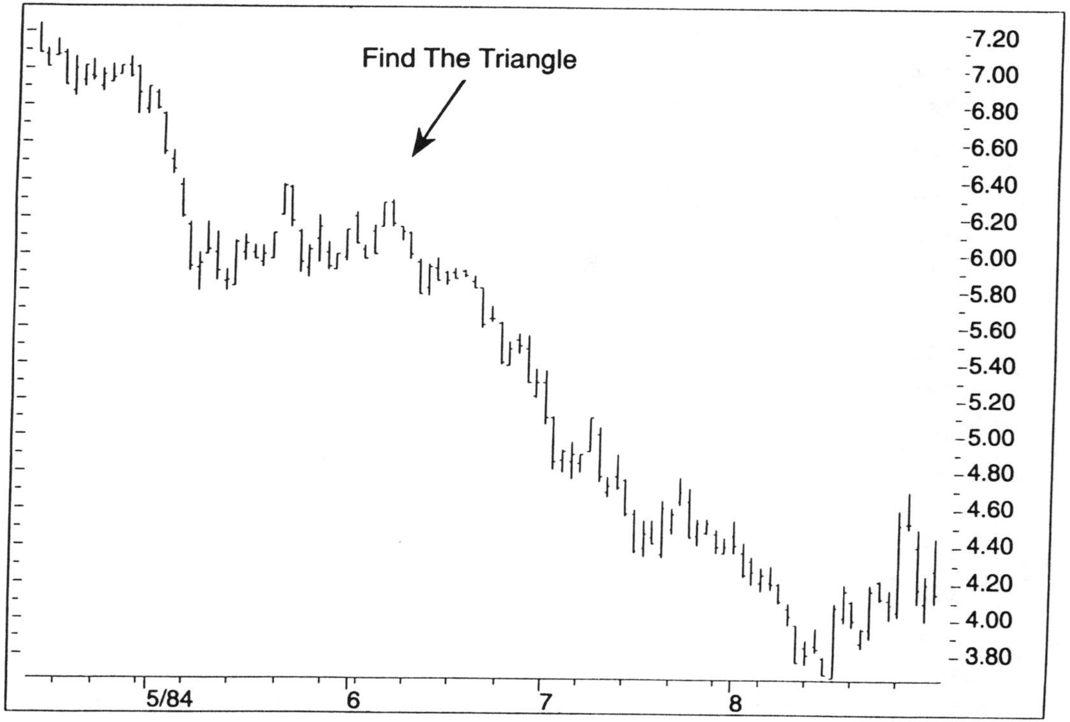

Find The Triangle

Figure 10–15

February 1985—Gold (Comex)

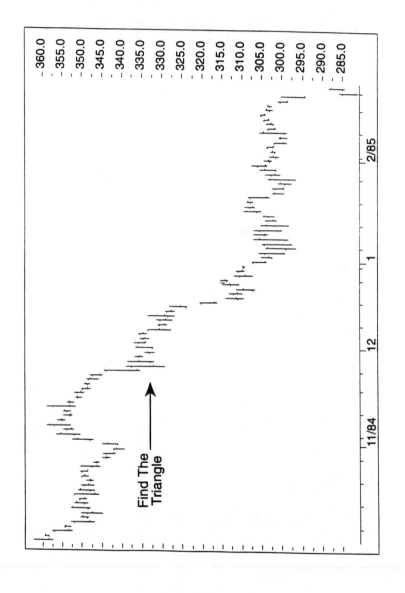

Figure 10-16

December 1989—Gold (Comex)

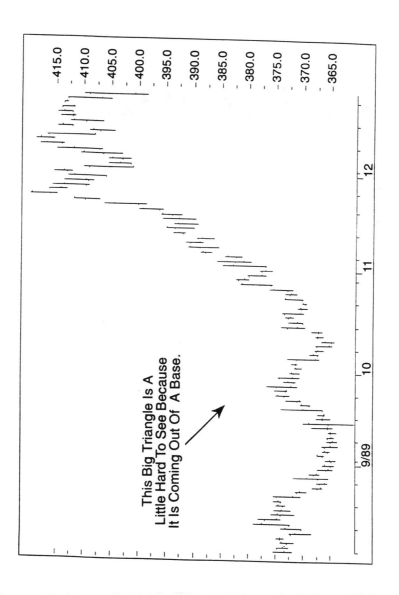

This Big Triangle Is A
Little Hard To See Because
It Is Coming Out Of A Base.

Figure 10—17

March 1983—Corn

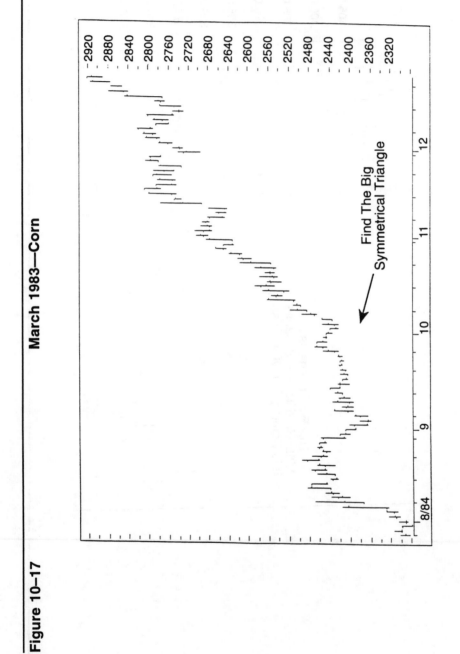

Find The Big
Symmetrical Triangle

Figure 10–18

December 1984—Corn

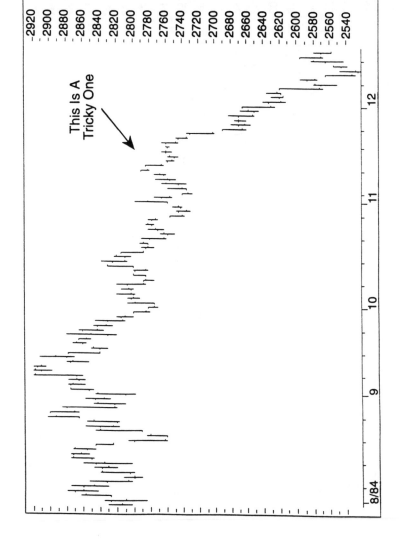

87

Figure 10–19

October 1990—Crude Oil

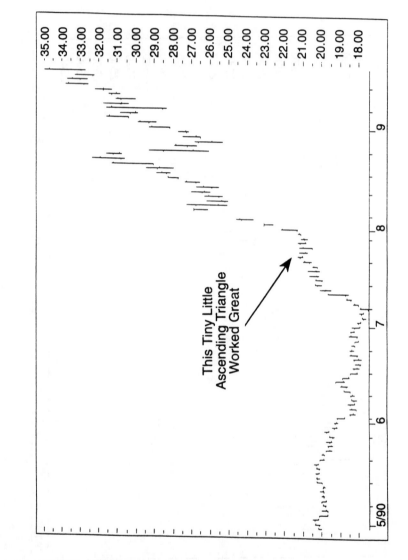

This Tiny Little
Ascending Triangle
Worked Great

Figure 10–20

December 1991–German Mark

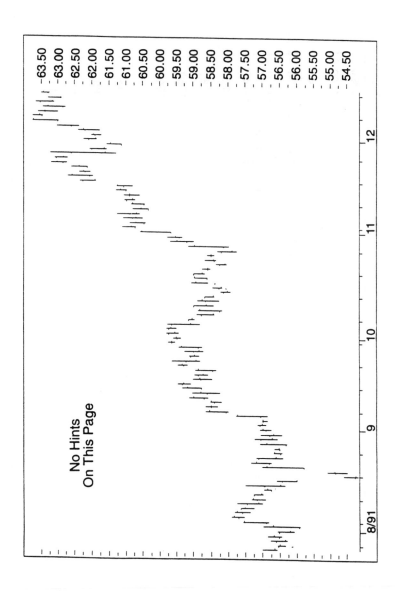

Figure 10–21

December 1993–Cocoa

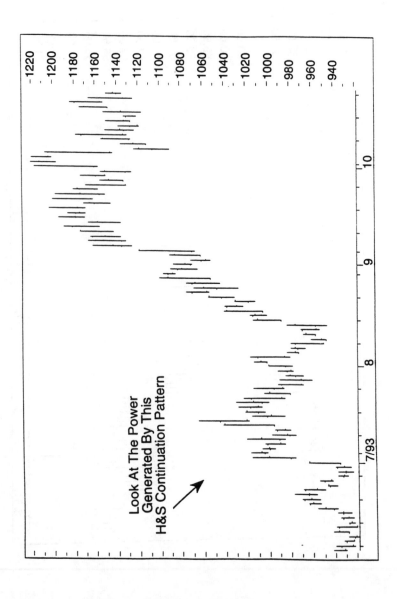

Look At The Power
Generated By This
H&S Continuation Pattern

Figure 10–22

December 1982–T-Bond

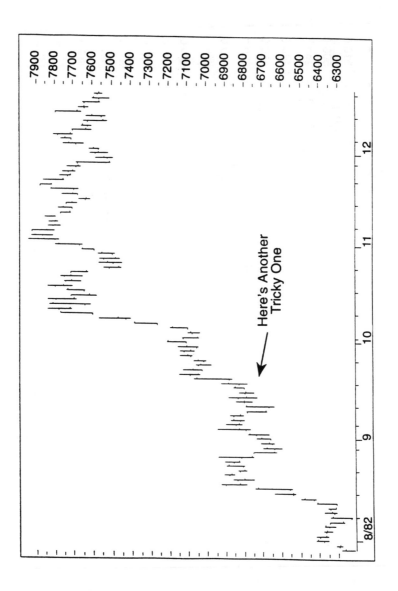

91

Figure 10–23

July 1993—Silver (Comex)

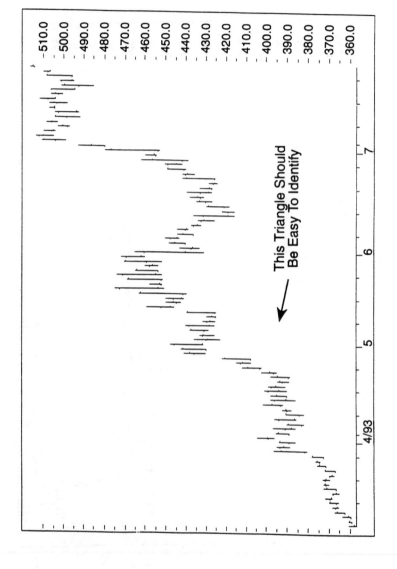

This Triangle Should
Be Easy To Identify

Teacher's Interpretations

Figure 10–1a

November 1991—Orange Juice

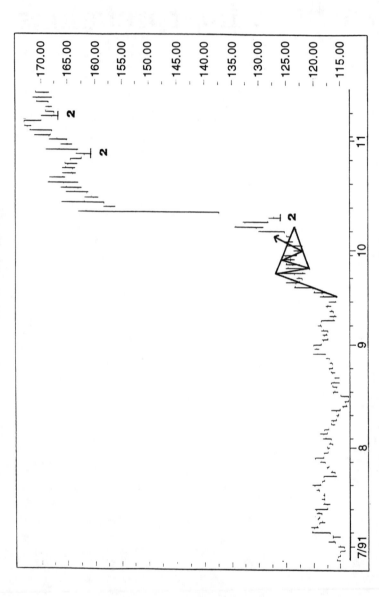

The market broke out of a long sideways consolidation in mid-September, then formed a perfect symmetrical triangle before blasting off. The trend was too steep to allow use of a logical trend line, so we relied on three distinct swing supports as the trend progressed.

Figure 10–2a

January 1988—Soybean Oil

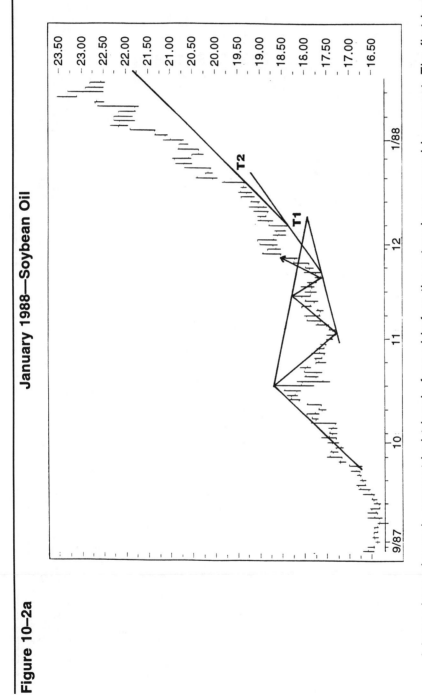

A large, lazy, six-week, symmetrical triangle formed before the uptrend progressed in earnest. The first logical trend line (T1) was eventually redrawn (T2). Notice how the stop alternated between the logical trend line and the swing supports.

Figure 10–3a

January 1988—Soybeans

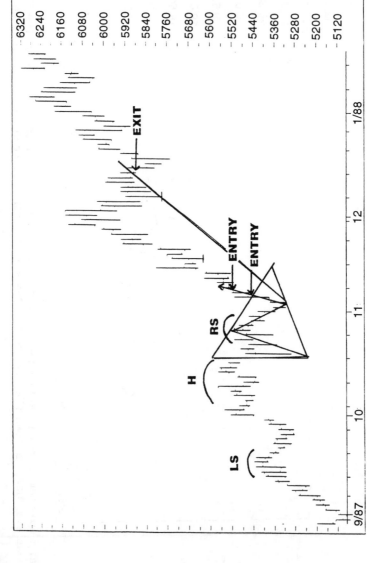

This trade may have been entered alternately either on the breakout of the symmetrical triangle that formed in the right shoulder, or one tick above the right shoulder. Two swing supports formed, one in mid-November, the other in early December. Until the second swing support formed, there was no way to draw a logical trend line. The exit came as a result of a break of the logical trend line.

96

Figure 10–4a

July 1993—Lumber

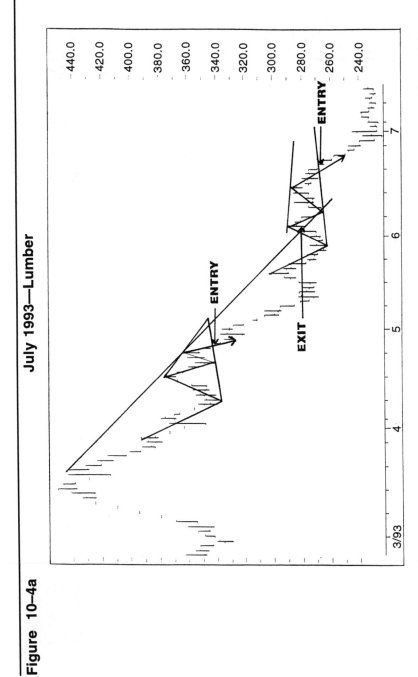

The triangle that formed in April was clear-cut. Immediately after the breakout, we were able to pick up a logical trend line that was already in place. After stopping out in early June, we were able to reenter the trend on the breakout of a second triangle that formed in June.

Figure 10-5a

January 1990—Lumber

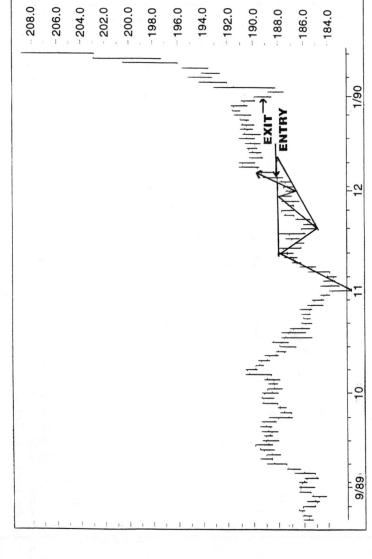

This ascending triangle failed to produce much profit. It may have been because the trend was not yet solidly established. Remember that ascending triangles work best when found high up in the trend. How would you have felt about missing the ensuing move? The correct answer is that it had nothing to do with your system. Your job is not to catch every move. Your job is to *follow your system.*

98

Figure 10–6a

June 1993—Japanese Yen

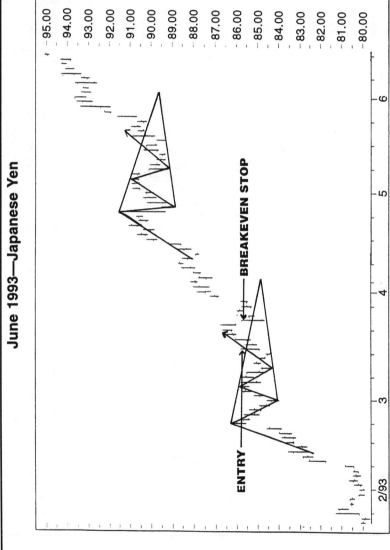

The two symmetrical triangles on this page are obvious. Remember to always move your stop to breakeven on the fourth day after entry.

99

Figure 10–7a

March 1993—Japanese Yen

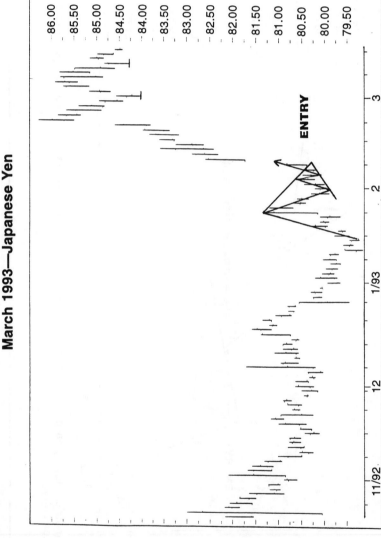

Even though this market was just turning from bear to bull, the powerful thrust in mid-January should have alerted you to a possible change in trend. There was essentially no place for a stop until swing supports developed much higher up. That shouldn't concern you. My research shows that in all but a very small percentage of cases, after a powerful move, the first retracement will be followed by a test of the high, which allows a swing support to develop.

Figure 10-8a

December 1991—Japanese Yen

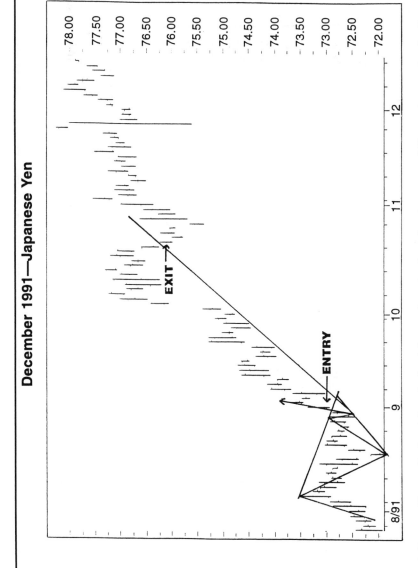

If you look carefully, you'll see that a triangle had formed and a breakout occurred three days prior to the one I have indicated. The first breakout failed, and you would have been stopped out at the apex on the following day. At that point, you would have had to redraw the triangle and reenter on a breakout of the new triangle. This is not an infrequent occurrence. Always be ready to reenter if the pattern still exists.

101

Figure 10–9a

March 1988—Japanese Yen

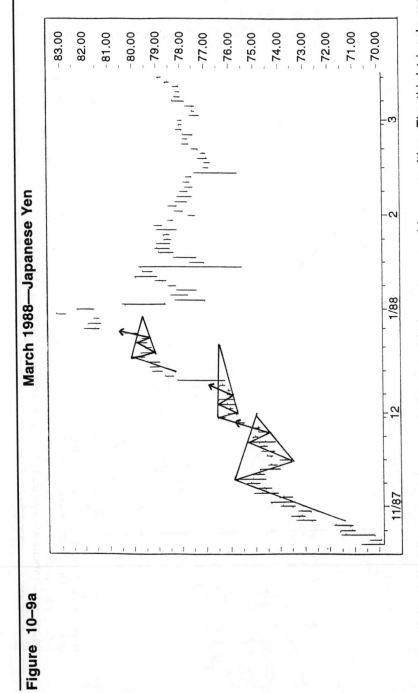

The second triangle in the series would have enabled you to pyramid your position. The third triangle resulted in a break-even trade, per the four-day rule.

Figure 10–10a

December 1982—Coffee 'C'

A clear-cut ascending triangle formed, continuing the trend.

Figure 10–11a

December 1985—Coffee 'C'

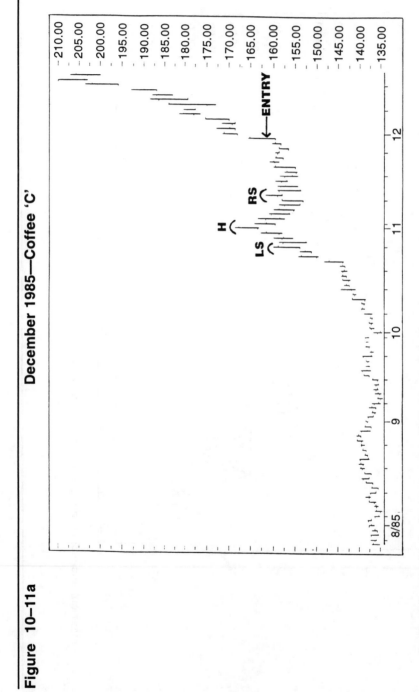

Another fine example demonstrating the power of the head-and-shoulders continuation pattern.

Figure 10–12a

December 1988—Coffee 'C'

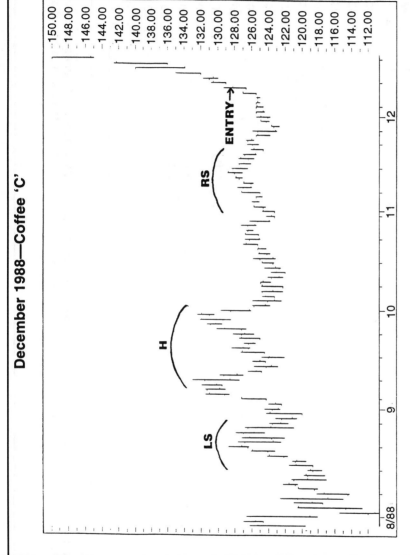

One might have taken this trade in mid-November and then had to reenter in early December. You can see, however, that perseverance would have paid off.

Figure 10–13a

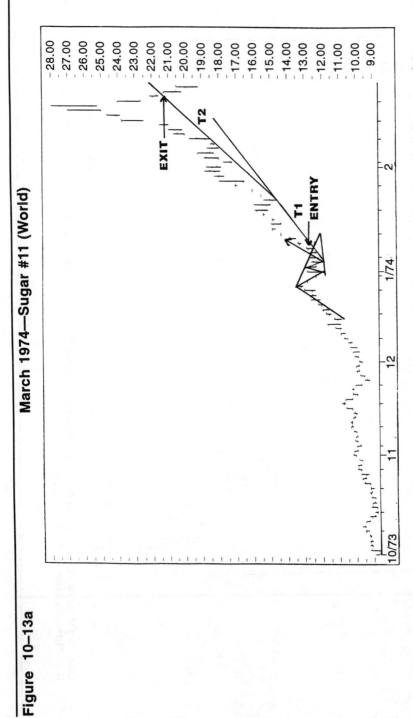

March 1974—Sugar #11 (World)

Notice how the logical trend line needed to be redrawn as support points developed. It is unusual to see a strong market give way so suddenly. The trailing stop under the logical trend line allowed us to lock in substantial profits.

Figure 10-14a

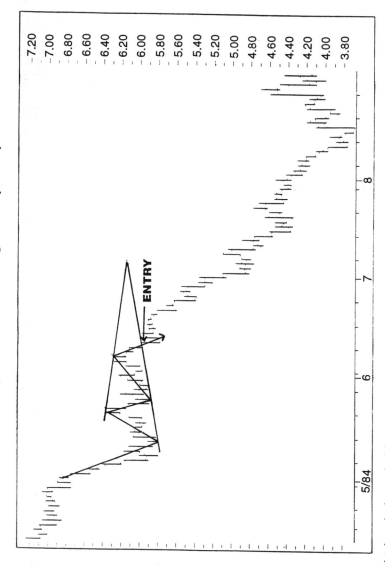

September 1984—Sugar #11 (World)

Here a symmetrical triangle is traded in a downtrend.

107

Figure 10–15a

February 1985—Gold (Comex)

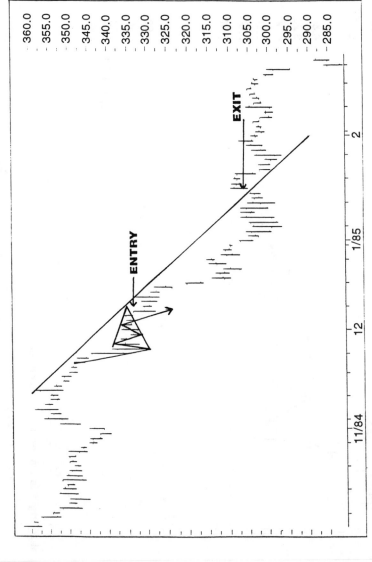

Tight little triangles like this are referred to as "dynamite" triangles. Because risk at entry is extremely low, these are my favorites. The logical trend line locked in profits. A swing resistance point in late December would have taken command of the stop for a couple of days. Can you find it?

Figure 10–16a

December 1989—Gold (Comex)

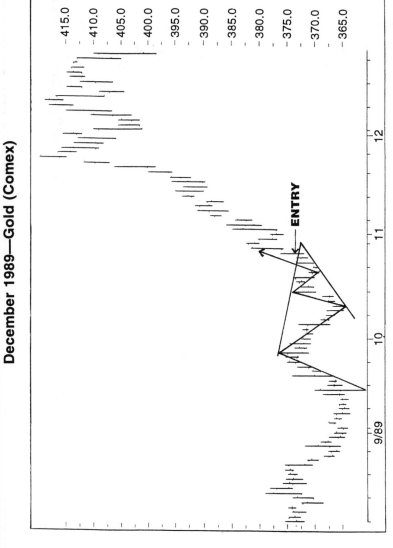

A symmetrical triangle formed coming out of the base.

Figure 10–17a

March 1983—Corn

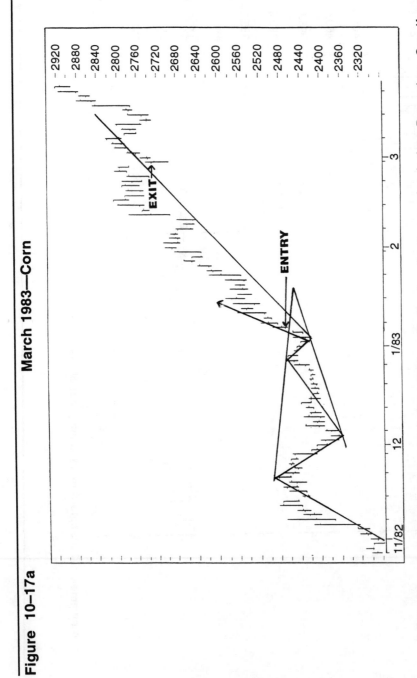

This triangle could have been drawn in earlier, with the breakout occurring in late December. See if you can find it and draw it in for practice.

110

Figure 10–18a

December 1984—Corn

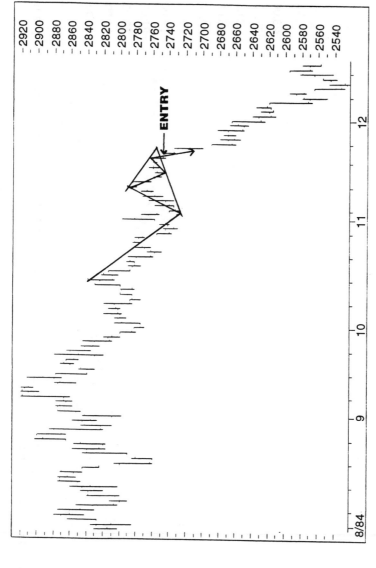

This pattern was difficult to see because it was part of a greater congestion pattern. Actually, a head-and-shoulders continuation pattern in a downtrend was in place. Remember: That trade is considered optional for more aggressive traders. Draw in the pattern for practice. You'll see that the entry below the right shoulder was nearly identical to the breakout of the symmetrical triangle.

111

Figure 10–19a

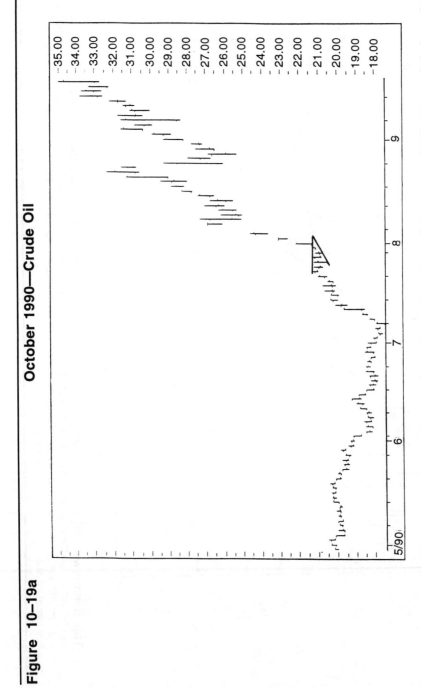

October 1990—Crude Oil

Notice how, when this ascending triangle formed, the market was still in a low volatility stage. It is less risky to enter the market during that stage.

Figure 10–20a

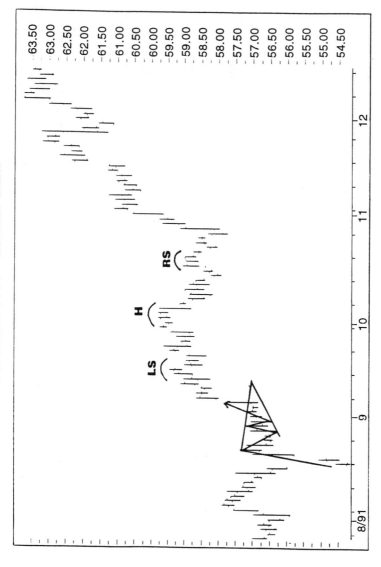

December 1991—German Mark

How well did you do in identifying these two patterns? Don't be too concerned if you didn't find them. I purposely selected a difficult example to prepare you for the real world. The more you practice, the more easily you will spot the
patterns.

113

Figure 10–21a

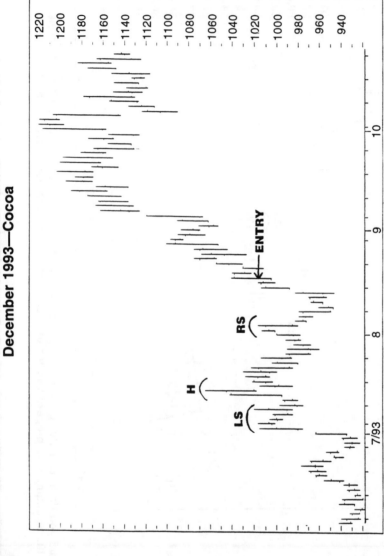

December 1993—Cocoa

Another example of the power of the head-and-shoulders continuation pattern. Unfortunately, this powerful pattern is rarely found. However, when you recognize one, you have good reason to be excited.

Figure 10–22a

December 1982—T-Bond

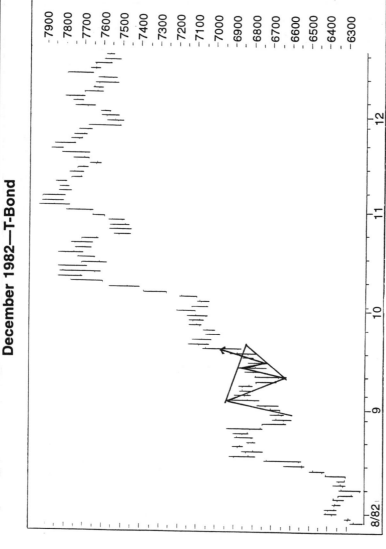

It looked as though the market was going to form a head-and-shoulders continuation pattern, but the underlying trend was so strong that the right shoulder never completed.

115

Figure 10–23a

July 1993—Silver (Comex)

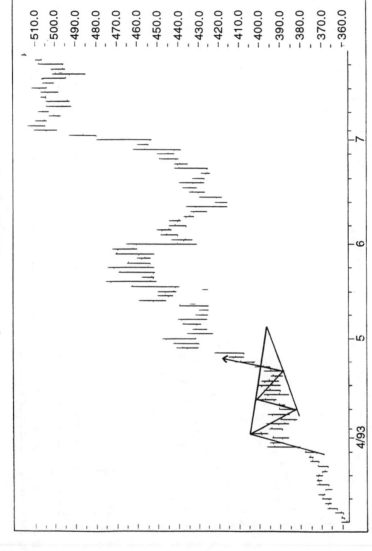

The patterns don't get much clearer than this one.

Quick Summary

To Go Long

Trend filters:	40 Day M.A. = flat or rising.
	18 Day M.A. = rising.
Entry patterns:	Symmetrical triangle.
	Ascending triangle.
	Head-and-shoulders continuation pattern.
Initial stop:	S.T.—Apex.
	A.T.— Bisected Angle.
	H&S—one-half distance to the neckline or $400.
Money management stop:	$400.
Break-even stop:	When profit = twice initial risk or fourth day after entry.
Trailing stop:	One tick below the closer of: swing supports power of two or logical trend line.

To Go Short

Trend filters:	40 Day M.A.—flat or declining.
	18 Day M.A.—declining.
Entry patterns:	Symmetrical triangle.
Initial stop:	Apex.
Money management stop:	$400.
Break-even stop:	When profit = twice initial risk or fourth day after entry.
Trailing stop:	One tick above the closer of swing resistance points power of two or logical trend line.

SECTION THREE

Deeper into
Pattern Research

You are now ready to explore chart patterns in greater detail. When you finish this section, you will have a thorough knowledge of classical chart patterns based on never-before-published, original research. **Note:** *This section, comprising mostly statistical research, is not light reading. Chapters 11–15 are not mandatory; you may, if you wish, skip to Chapter 16, which summarizes the results of the research.*

C h a p t e r   1 1

Double Bottoms
and
Double Tops

> *This chapter begins with a chartist's quiz. Test yourself on your knowledge of chart patterns and their implications. Then, learn the truth about double bottoms and double tops—two of the most easily recognized patterns. Are they worth trading?*

In Section Two, you learned a simple way to get started using the PPS approach. In this section, we are going to examine those patterns in more detail, as well as quite a few other classical patterns. Some of the patterns are ones you may have assumed were profitable, but may not be. Other patterns will be used in ways you are unaccustomed with. By chapter's end, you will be an expert on classical chart patterns as they apply to futures trading. In addition, you will have added several new entry patterns to your PPS arsenal and will have mastered all the mechanical aspects of the PPS entries and exits.

But before we begin to look at the statistical research, let's have a little fun. I want you to take what I call the Chartist's Quiz. If my guess is correct, you'll be amazed how *little* you actually know about chart patterns—especially when forced to make intelligent trading decisions based on that knowledge. Mark your answers on a separate piece of paper. The answers will be given at the end of the chapter.

Chartist's Quiz

1. After a double bottom has formed, what is the probability that prices will reach their objective?

   A. 78.5 percent
   B. 62.5 percent
   C. 51.5 percent
   D. 42.5 percent

2. A double bottom is generally more reliable if the second bottom does not drop below the first bottom.

   A. True
   B. False

3. If the double bottom also breaks a downtrend line, the pattern is more likely to be successful.

   A. True
   B. False

4. Assume that a double top forms over 15 days. On the day prices break the neckline, you sell an out-of-the-money call with 15 days remaining before expiration, having a strike price equal to the highest point of the double top. What is the probability that the call will expire worthless?

   A. 49 percent
   B. 68 percent
   C. 85 percent
   D. 95 percent

5. Rectangles are reversal patterns what percentage of the time?

   A. 20
   B. 31
   C. 44
   D. 59

6. Head-and-shoulders tops are more likely to reach their objective than head-and-shoulders bottoms.

   A. True
   B. False

7. Ascending triangles occur in uptrends what percentage of the time?

   A. 46
   B. 68
   C. 84
   D. 93

8. Ascending triangles occur less frequently than symmetrical triangles.

   A. True
   B. False

9. Descending triangles should be traded as continuation patterns.

   A. True
   B. False

10. A symmetrical triangle will continue the trend what percentage of the time?

    A. 48
    B. 62
    C. 72
    D. 86

How well do you think you did? Take a guess at what you probably scored. After all, such an exercise is not unlike what you do when you trade. Don't you at least guess intuitively at the probable results of your trade?

Double Bottoms

Probably one of the first-learned and most often referred-to patterns is the double bottom. How often have you heard a financial commentator say something like, "It looks like the bonds are forming a double bottom"? What does he mean? He may not know—not exactly, anyway. So how are *you* supposed to know? But even more importantly, if the bonds did indeed form a double bottom, which we have yet to define, what are the implications? The commentator must surely think a double bottom offers some predictive value, or why would he bother to bring it to our attention?

Actually, conventional wisdom claims that once a double bottom has formed, prices will reach a minimum objective equal to the depth of the double bottom as measured from the breakout (see Figure 11–1).

Defining the Pattern

A double bottom consists of four swings: a continuation probe, a reaction, a test, and a completion swing (see Figure 11–2). I think everyone would agree with that. The following definitions, however, are my own, created out of necessity so that my analysis could be more precise and meaningful.

A "retracement" may occur after the pattern has formed but before the objective is reached. I have defined *retracement* as any move that violates the neckline.

I have defined *objective* as a price equal to the continuation probe measured from the neckline.

For a pattern to qualify as a double bottom, I require that the distance of the test, measured from the neckline, must be at least 85 percent of the continuation probe, also measured from the neckline, or vice versa. Therefore, the test may be slightly shorter or slightly longer than the continuation probe.

Finally, I require the pattern to be at least 10 days long in order to qualify as a double bottom.

**Figure 11–1   Double Bottom Objective
                            (Conventional Wisdom)**

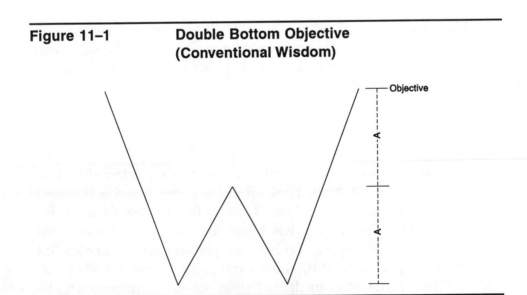

Figure 11–2   **Double Bottom Swings**

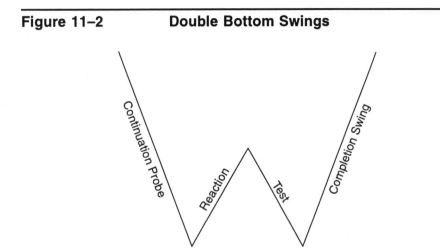

Methodology

Other criteria for my analysis included the following: Was the market in a major uptrend or downtrend when the bottom occurred? Upon completion of the pattern, was a trend line broken? This trend line may have been a minor downtrend while the major trend was up.

Completion of the pattern was measured and recorded. Completion refers to the maximum distance from the neckline that the move achieved before breaking support or a reasonable trend line. The pattern was called a success if completion was equal to or greater than the distance from the neckline to the bottom of the continuation probe. The number of days to completion was also recorded.

One final distinction was made. Double bottoms were one of two types (see Figure 11–3): Type A bottoms were less severe, a previous low having been lower than the peak in the double bottom. These usually occurred in a channeled downtrend and resulted in the breaking of the downtrend line. Type B bottoms formed after a severe washout and were distinct on the chart, the pattern in no way overlapping a previous low.

Results

In 30 markets over a 10-year period, I was able to identify and catalog 130 occurrences of double bottoms that conformed to the predefined parameters. With statistics on all of the double bottoms in hand, I then began to interrogate those statistics in search of market truths.

Figure 11–3   **Double Bottoms—Type A and B**

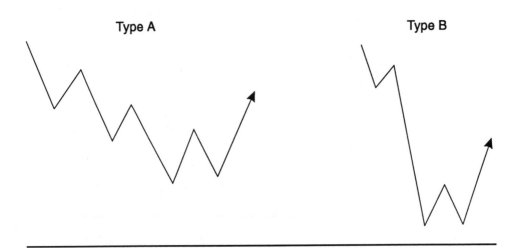

Question: How many double bottoms reached their objective before breaking significant support or a trend line?

Answer: 67, or 51.5 percent of the sample.

Question: Of the 67 successes, were either Type A or Type B double bottoms dominant?

Answer: No. They were approximately equally divided. My original assumption that one or the other type would show better forecasting ability proved incorrect.

Question: What percentage of double bottoms formed during downtrends?

Answer: One would expect that most double bottoms would be found in downtrends, and that did prove to be the case. From the sample, 80 formed during downtrends, 45 during uptrends, and 5 during broad trading ranges.

Question: Are those double bottoms that form within the context of a major uptrend more likely to be successful?

Answer: No. The success ratio during uptrends was only 53 percent, not statistically different from the entire sample.

Question: Can reliability be increased by requiring restrictions of the test probe?

Answer: No. The data showed test probes shorter in 80 cases, longer in 31 cases, and equal in 19 cases. Bottoms with the shorter test probe were successful 51.2 percent of the time; those with the longer test probe were successful 54.8 percent of the time; and those with a test probe of equal length were successful 47.4 percent of the time. Again, no statistically significant difference was found (see Figure 11–4).

Figure 11–4   **Double Bottoms—Different Length**
                        Test Probes

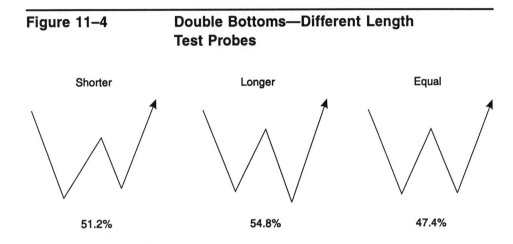

Shorter	Longer	Equal
51.2%	54.8%	47.4%

Question: Are double bottoms that require a longer time to form more reliable than those that form over a shorter period of time?

Answer: No. Of the 67 successful bottoms, I divided the sample into those whose formation consisted of 30 days or more and those whose formation consisted of less than 30 days. Only 16, or 39 percent, of the successful bottoms were 30 days or greater in length. This indicated that bottoms formed over a greater length of time are no more successful than those taking less time to form (see Figure 11–5).

Question: If the completion of a double bottom also breaks a downtrend line, is the pattern more likely to be successful?

Answer: No. Of the 101 bottoms that coincidentally broke a downtrend line, only 48, or 47.5 percent, went on to success—even less than the 51.5 percent shown in the overall sample (see Figure 11–6).

Figure 11–5   **Double Bottoms—Shorter and**
                        Longer Formation Periods

10-30 Days   30-50 Days

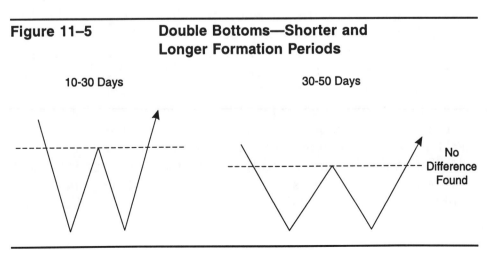

No Difference Found

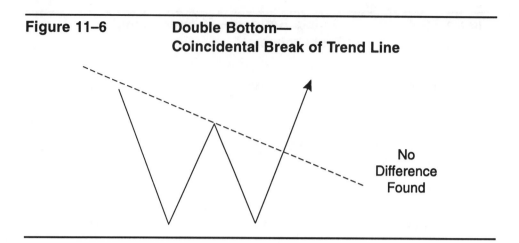

Figure 11–6   **Double Bottom—**
Coincidental Break of Trend Line

No
Difference
Found

By now, I had nearly concluded that my data on double bottoms proved absolutely nothing and had been a gargantuan waste of time. But wait...there was still a column of figures I had not yet examined: retracements.

You will remember that I defined a retracement as any move that violates the neckline subsequent to the completion of the pattern. To my amazement, I found that in 50 of the 130 occurrences, there was no retracement whatsoever! In other words, the market just kept on going up without looking back. But what percentage of those turned into successes? Of the 50, 35, or 70 percent, were successes. Of the 80 bottoms that exhibited retracements, only 32, or 40 percent, were successes. That's a statistically significant difference; there is no question about it. Those double bottoms that exhibit no retracement are *almost twice as likely* to be successful as those that do retrace.

Conclusions

There are many chart traders who, upon discovering a double bottom, believe they have identified the beginning of a new trend. The results of my research should lead them to be more cautious. It seems that while the double bottom successfully identifies the turn in trend, it may not offer the best place to enter the trade. This is because the turning point tends to be treacherous—six out of every 10 trades will be subject to one or more retracements below the neckline before continuing in the expected direction.

The double bottom can truly be called a reversal pattern, however. The prior trend was changed 64 percent of the time once a double bottom was formed. The remaining 36 percent of the time, the double bottom failed to reach its objective, and the prior trend continued in force.

Therefore, a trader would be wise to cover short positions upon encountering this pattern; should he have other reasons—fundamental, seasonal, cyclical, and so on—for expecting higher prices, he may consider establishing a long position. However, because of the high potential for immediate retracement, one might instead consider outright calls, vertical call spreads, or even the sale of puts.

Although the double bottom was not one of the final patterns chosen to become part of the PPS Trading System, I am sharing my analysis of the research data with you so that you will recognize the limitations of this very common pattern.

Double Tops

Double tops are a rather common phenomenon. Of the pattern, Edwards and Magee said, "It is referred to by name perhaps more often than any other chart pattern by traders who possess a smattering of technical lingo but little organized knowledge of technical facts." I couldn't agree more. Those who try to pick tops often feel that the very *existence* of a double top is a good reason to short the market. More often than not, this strategy produces losses. The reason is that the double top often turns out to be no more than what Elliott termed a "flat": a corrective pattern not distinguishable from a double top until long after the fact.

Defining the Pattern

A double top is really nothing more than a double bottom turned upside down. But in an effort to be complete, I will review the definition, this time in the context of a double top. The double top consists of four distinct swings: a continuation probe, a reaction, a test, and a completion swing.

After the pattern has formed, but before its objective is reached, a retracement may occur; I define a retracement as any move that violates the neckline. The objective is equal to the continuation probe measured from the neckline. To qualify as a double top, I have required that the distance of the test, measured from the neckline, must be at least 85 percent of the continuation probe, also measured from the neckline, or vice versa. Therefore, the test may be slightly shorter or slightly longer than the continuation probe.

Finally, the pattern requires a minimum of 10 days in development in order to qualify as a double top.

Methodology

Having gained knowledge from the study of double bottoms, the study of double tops took a new direction. First, the test that distinguished between Type A and Type B double bottoms was eliminated in the study of double tops. Second, no distinction was made as to whether a trend line was broken. Instead, three new studies were added to the research. In question and answer format, the results of these three studies follow.

Results

Question: What percentage of the completed double tops retraced to the area of the neckline?

Answer: Interestingly, it was found that in 82 percent of the cases there was a reaction to or in the general vicinity of the neckline. Because of this, one might suppose that one should wait for that reaction and then enter the short position when the new downtrend resumes. Unfortunately, many of the very big winners were found not to retrace at all!

Question: What percentage of the patterns actually reversed the prior trend?

Answer: In only 28 percent of the cases did the double top actually reverse the trend. The other 72 percent of the time, the trend eventually continued higher. This statistic proves—quite emphatically—that most of the time a double top will not reverse an uptrend.

Of course, eventually an uptrend will come to an end; when it does, you might find a double top at its pinnacle. But you are just as likely to find another pattern.

Question: After a double top has completed, and a given period of time has elapsed, are prices generally higher, lower, or in the same vicinity as the neckline?

Answer: To answer this question, I measured the width of the double top (time) and added that horizontally to the point of breakout (see Figure 11–7). In 37.5 percent of the cases, prices were in the same general vicinity at that point in time. In 47.2 percent of the cases, prices were lower. In 15.3 percent of the cases, prices were higher. These statistics could be invaluable when considering an option strategy. For example, assume that a double top has formed, taking 15 days to complete. There is an option series expir-

Figure 11–7   **Double Top—Level of Prices after a Period of Time Equal to the Width of the Double Top**

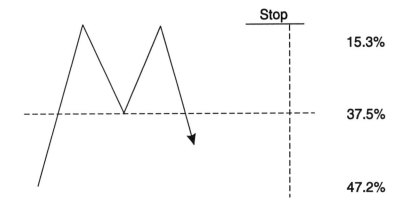

Stop

15.3%

37.5%

47.2%

ing in 15 days. If a trader were to sell out-of-the-money calls, there would be an 84.7 percent chance that they would expire worthless, allowing him to keep the premium.

Conclusions

The research clearly shows that it is unwise to attempt to trade double tops as reversal formations in major uptrends. In most cases (72 percent of the time), the former uptrend will eventually continue, thereby eliminating the potential size of any profit from a short position. Another problem is that very often (82 percent of the time), a sharp retracement will carry prices back to the general area of the neckline (often above it), subjecting the position to being stopped out.

On the other hand, option strategies could prove profitable, given that a majority of the time (84.7 percent), prices will not move higher over the near term (the approximate time that it took the double top to form).

The most exciting results, however, were revealed when I examined only those double tops that occurred within a major downtrend (thus reversing only a minor uptrend). Here, results were startlingly different: Not only was a very high percentage of the trades profitable, but the average profit per trade was very high as well. By using the double top only on those occasions when it appears within a major downtrend, a trader can expect to find a low-risk entry for a short position. The double top, used in this way, was eventually to become part of the PPS System.

Chapter 12

Head-and-Shoulders
Tops and Bottoms

> *You learned how to use the head-and-shoulders top as a con-*
> *tinuation pattern in PPS Fast Start. What else should you*
> *know about these patterns?*

Head-and-Shoulders Tops

Triple tops are extremely rare in commodities, and their implications appear to be identical to head-and-shoulders tops. Therefore,
I combined the two patterns in my study.

Methodology

With these patterns, the developmental period was restricted to 10–
75 days. In the head-and-shoulders tops, shoulders were required to
achieve a height of between 25 percent and 50 percent of the
height of the head. For triple tops, both shoulders were required to
achieve a height 75–125 percent of the height of the head. For both
patterns, the distance between valleys was required to be nearly
equal, in keeping with cyclicality considerations responsible for pattern formation. The objective was defined as the distance from the

top of the head to the midpoint of the neckline. A time requirement in which to meet the objective was defined as a period of
time equal to the width of the pattern.

Results

Question: Is the head-and-shoulders top tradable?

Answer: No. Under the requirements imposed, which were
similar to other patterns tested, a very low percentage of trades was
successful. Those requirements were that the trade could be implemented with a low-risk fixed stop and that a reward of three to one
was achievable.

Question: Does the head-and-shoulders top reverse the previous
uptrend?

Answer: Yes. Approximately 64 percent of the time the objective was reached within the given time period and, by that definition, the trend was successfully reversed. These figures are strong
enough to take into consideration. For example, if one were long,
one should liquidate upon a break of the neckline or risk a 64 percent chance that prices would eventually fall to the objective. Also,
option strategies may be implemented given the 64 percent probability that prices will achieve a certain level within a specified period of time (the width of the pattern).

Head-and-Shoulders Bottoms

Methodology

The methodology applied was the same as for the head-and-shoulders and triple tops.

Results

Quite unexpectedly, I found the frequency of occurrence of these
patterns to be much greater than those of their counterpart tops.
Head-and-shoulders bottoms are twice as common as head-and-
shoulders tops, and triple bottoms are 10 times as common as triple
tops!

Question: Are head-and-shoulders bottoms tradeable?

Answer: Only if you want to go broke. Their performance was
even worse than head-and-shoulders tops.

Question: Does the head-and-shoulders bottom reverse the previous downtrend?

Answer: Only about half the time. More precisely, the down-trend was reversed and the objective reached only 51.4 percent of the time. This should come as quite a shock to that large majority of traders who become excitedly bullish when they notice one of these patterns developing.

Because of the much larger sample size of head-and-shoulders bottoms and triple bottoms, I was able to separate the two and do some additional testing. Although some caution should be given because of the relatively small sample size, it did appear that significantly better results were produced by the triple bottoms.

Conclusions

These findings are certainly a testimonial to the power of trends. Even in the face of the most powerful reversal patterns known, the trend continues in better than half of all cases. The objective was reached in these bottoming patterns 56.3 percent of the time. It should be noted that a small or shallow pattern may propel prices to the objective without price having breached the overall down-trend. The study reveals the impotence of the pattern: In 43.7 percent of the cases, the pattern lacked the power to propel prices to the objective, let alone reverse the downtrend.

Conclusions: Head-and-Shoulders Tops and Bottoms; Triple Tops and Bottoms

The results of my research debunk the popular myth that one of the best ways to make money is to wait for a head-and-shoulders bottom and then buy or to wait for a head-and-shoulders top and then sell. Either approach falls into the categories known as bottom picking or top picking, and should be avoided.

Of the two approaches, however, one is more likely to profit by attempting to sell a head-and-shoulders top. While I could not find a low-risk strategy that would work, that is not to say that a different type of strategy could not be devised that would be profitable.

While the head-and-shoulders top, found within an uptrend, is not used in the PPS Trading System, we may be able to utilize information about it. For example, what if we encounter a small, highly reliable symmetrical triangle formed at the neckline of the right shoulder? We can now combine the information we have compiled on the two different patterns. First, we know the probabilities of the symmetrical triangle. But we now have further information: We know that once the neckline is broken on the head-and-shoulders top, there is a two-thirds chance that the objective will be reached.

Head-and-shoulders bottoms must be a graveyard for the average chart-oriented trader. There are three reasons why: First, these patterns are encountered twice as often as the head-and-shoulders top; second, most traders prefer to buy rather than to sell; third, the record of success of these patterns is far worse than head-and-shoulders tops.

Regarding triple bottoms, the outlook is somewhat brighter. Here, the objective is reached a significantly larger percentage of the time. But it is quite possible that triple bottoms are, on average, shallower than head-and-shoulders bottoms. That would make the distance to the objective shorter and the objective more easily achieved. Again, the relatively small data sample taints any conclusions that might be drawn.

A few comments regarding strategy are appropriate. Although I could not find a low-risk strategy that was successful with these patterns, I did create one strategy that yielded relatively good results. Using that strategy, the stop was placed above the right shoulder in the case of a top, and below the right shoulder in the case of a bottom. This stop placement greatly increased the percentage of winning trades. The downside was a great increase in risk.

Chapter 13

Triangles

> *Triangles are core patterns for PPS. You learned how to use both the ascending triangle and symmetrical triangle in PPS Fast Start. This chapter will present more detail on those patterns, as well as introduce you to a new pattern: the descending triangle.*

Symmetrical Triangles

If you read Chapter 7, Fast-Start Entries, you can identify a symmetrical triangle and you know how to use it. In this chapter, you'll learn even more about this pattern.

Interestingly, the symmetrical triangle is one of the patterns where my research (conducted on commodities) produced results in stark contrast to Edwards and Magee's (conducted on stocks). Edwards and Magee expressed a definite wariness toward this pattern, stating that "symmetrical triangles are subject to false moves to a far greater extent than head-and-shoulders or any other formations" and also that "no technical chart formation is 100 percent reliable, and of all, the symmetrical triangle is the worst offender." While they classified the pattern as a reversal pattern, in the same chapter they stated that the pattern was more apt to signal consolidation.

Are symmetrical triangles reversal formations or continuation patterns? Should we be alert to a trend change, or should we expect the trend to continue? My research showed that, in commodities, symmetrical triangles *overwhelmingly* resolve themselves in the direction of the trend. In fact, of the 118 triangles identified, 102, or 86.4 percent, broke out in the direction of the trend. You can see why the symmetrical triangle was chosen as one of the core patterns in the PPS Trading System.

Methodology

The pattern was required to be at least 10 days long but not more than 50. It had to stand out cleanly on the chart, not be part of some larger pattern or trading range. The triangle could, however, form as a right shoulder of an incomplete head-and-shoulders top or bottom. Initial risk was to the apex. Profit or loss was determined by the following stop placement rules: The stop was moved to breakeven when profit was three times the initial risk; after that, the trade continued in force until either a swing support or a reasonable trend line was breached. A trade was considered a success only if the profit was at least three times the risk.

Results

Given our definition of success, what percentage of trades taken in the direction of the trend were profitable compared to those taken countertrend? In other words, is the pattern more powerful as a continuation pattern or as a reversal pattern? The answer is: Success is 50 percent more likely if the triangle is only traded in the direction of the trend. Specifically, 37.3 percent of the trades were successes with the trend compared to only 25 percent countertrend. Looking at the percentage of trades that were profitable, 51 percent were profitable in the direction of the trend while only 31.3 percent were profitable countertrend. Given this information, we can conclude that we should only consider trading those symmetrical triangles that break in the direction of the trend—which, coincidentally, five out of six do—and ignore those triangles that resolve countertrend.

Will this approach produce profits? The results were eye-opening. After factoring in slippage and commission estimates, I found that 51 percent of the trades were profitable, and the average profit was seven times larger than the average loss!

There was still more about symmetrical triangles that I wanted to know. I wondered if profitability was affected by the size of the triangle. I divided the entire data set into two halves—those 10–29 days long and those 30–50 days long. I found virtually no difference in the number of successes: The small triangles produced 37.7 percent; the large, 36.4 percent. Would larger triangles beget larger moves? To find out, I looked at the top 15 most profitable trades. Neither small nor large triangles dominated as the progenitor. While I was also curious about whether some markets were more reliable than others, given the limited number of trades in each market, no statistically significant conclusions could be drawn.

To summarize the results: 1) Five out of every six symmetrical triangles resolve in the direction of the trend; 2) Symmetrical triangles should only be traded in the direction of the trend; and 3) By limiting losses to a breach of the apex, a very high risk/reward ratio can be achieved, while allowing approximately half of all trades to be profitable.

Essentially, the symmetrical triangle allows us a low-risk opportunity to establish a position in a trending market whose trend is highly likely to continue.

Ascending Triangles

If you have read Chapter 7, Fast-Start Entries, you already know what the ascending triangle looks like and how to use it. There is very little to add here. You should remember that the research showed that the post-triangle thrust is generally much weaker in the ascending triangle than in the symmetrical triangle (the average profit per trade was only two-thirds as great).

One other important feature was not mentioned earlier: The ascending triangle should not be used in downtrends. Actual testing showed that, in downtrends, only 20 percent of the trades were profitable, compared to 43.2 percent in uptrends. In addition, the profit per trade in downtrends was only one-third as high as uptrends. It is important to remember that this pattern is more reliable when found in a well-established uptrend, as opposed to one still in its embryonic stages.

Descending Triangles

A first cousin to the ascending triangle, the descending triangle appears simply as an ascending triangle turned upside down. Together, these two patterns—the right-angled triangles—account for

42 percent of all triangles, the remaining 58 percent being symmetrical triangles.

There are at least two reasons that could account for their rarity relative to symmetrical triangles. The first may simply be a matter of definition: At some point, a skewed symmetrical triangle could be classified as a right-angled triangle, and vice versa. Another distinct possibility, and one that I would favor, is that commodities by nature are more volatile than stocks. Thus, rallies or declines that approach the horizontal boundary line frequently break through by enough to disrupt the potential pattern.

Unlike Edwards and Magee, I distinguished between descending triangles that formed subsequent to a price decline and those that formed subsequent to a price rally, labeling them Type A and Type B respectively (see Figure 13–1). This distinction proved important. The bisected angle strategy (see Chapter 7) was applied to all cases.

Figure 13–1   Descending Triangles—Type A and Type B

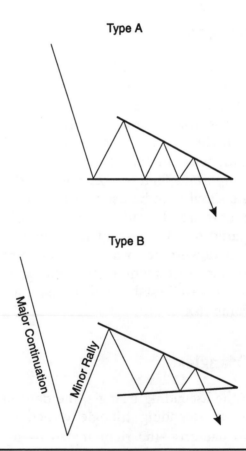

Type A

Type B

Results

In the sample, Type A and Type B descending triangles were nearly equally distributed; yet trades emanating from Type Bs were almost three times more likely to be winners. The wins were larger, and the losses were smaller. Again, Type Bs were the type that reversed a previous minor uptrend within a major downtrend. Type As acted as continuation patterns and were preceded by a previous major downtrend.

The conclusion is that descending triangles should be traded only as reversal patterns—they make good tops. But they should *not* be traded as continuation patterns. It appears they do not have the power to propel prices down and sufficiently away from the pattern. Instead, prices frequently bob back up into the pattern, disallowing any possible low-risk entry. Actual statistics showed that Type A patterns (continuation) were successful only 18 percent of the time and were, overall, unprofitable. Type B patterns (reversal) were successful 52 percent of the time and displayed profitability approximately equal to that of the ascending triangle.

Ascending Triangles Revisited

After completing the research on descending triangles, in which Type A and Type B patterns were examined separately, I then revisited the ascending triangles, applying these same Type A and Type B definitions. One would certainly expect the results to mirror those of the descending triangles. Indeed, Edwards and Magee gave no indication that we could expect otherwise, stating that "descending triangles are created by market conditions that are just the reverse of those responsible for ascending patterns" and that "their implications are equally strong." So I was astonished that my results were so contrary.

The first inconsistency was that, among ascending triangles, Type As and Type Bs were not equally distributed, as they had been with the descending triangles. The data showed that 88 percent of the sample consisted of Type As (uptrend-continuation). Trading results from this subset were excellent, as had been shown before. In contrast, trading results from the Type Bs (downtrend-reversal) subset were poor: Only 20 percent were winners, and overall results were barely profitable.

Right-Angled Triangles:
Thoughts on Resolving the Conflict

If, indeed, ascending and descending triangles are merely two sides of the same coin—as Edwards and Magee would have us believe—then why, using the same trading strategy, do the results vary so dramatically? Why is it that my results show that ascending triangles work well as continuation patterns, yet poorly as reversal patterns; while descending triangles work well as reversal patterns, yet poorly as continuation patterns? One would expect all right-angled triangles to either work well as continuation patterns or as reversal patterns. Isn't a descending triangle simply an ascending triangle held up to a mirror? If you say yes, then would you also agree that a downtrend is simply an uptrend held up to a mirror? I would disagree—and therein may lie our answer.

Professional traders know that bull markets are easier to trade than bear markets. The reason has to do with volatility. Bull markets simply act differently than bear markets—they are more orderly. Bear markets find prices crashing one day only to be followed by a vicious rally the next. Why is this? It is because the motivation to sell (fear) is a far stronger emotion than the motivation to buy (greed). Bull markets are thus ruled by greed; whereas, bear markets are ruled by fear. It is these emotions that color and characterize price movements differently in uptrends and downtrends, so we should not be surprised to see our patterns affected as well.

Let's apply this logic to our results. Ascending triangles work well in uptrends as continuation patterns. Initially, the market becomes overbought, and prices are turned back the first time. Eventually, demand enters, and prices soon reach their old high, where they are turned back by supply once again. But this time, buying comes in at a higher level, supporting the fact that buyers are indeed coming into the market. Prices eventually break through the resistance at the old high—as those who attempted to short now buy to cover their short positions. It is these dynamics that propel prices powerfully out of the pattern.

The dynamics of a descending triangle in a downtrend, however, are different. Now, sellers are in control. Prices drop to a point where they are considered oversold. A few brash buyers attempt to bottom fish and do some tentative buying. Because most of the bearish traders have already sold, prices rally quite easily. The higher price, however, attracts sellers once again, and the price retreats to the low. Because the market has shown some support at that price, more buyers come tentatively into the market. This time the rally is weak, as the passage of time and bearish fundamentals attract sellers again. Prices break through the old low. Tentative buyers, who bought at the support price, now liquidate their long positions.

So where is the difference? The difference is that in the latter case, selling is likely to quickly dry up; most sellers who wanted to sell have already done so. Others will wait for a rally to get a better price. But as soon as buyers, who are waiting on the sidelines, perceive that selling pressure is lessening, they will again attempt to bottom fish, and prices may rally sharply. In the former case (uptrend), hordes of buyers are likely to come into the market once a new high has been firmly established. So, the uptrend is more likely to continue for a while. How do we apply this knowledge to our trading? Trade ascending triangles as continuation patterns in uptrends, but do not trade descending triangles as continuation patterns in downtrends.

Finally, let's look at the case of a descending triangle in an uptrend. Why does the descending triangle have the power to reverse an uptrend, even though the ascending triangle could not reverse a downtrend? Again, the answer lies in the differing motivations of buyers and sellers.

When a descending triangle forms in an uptrend, it is likely that far more speculators are long than were short during the downtrend. This is because speculators generally have a bullish orientation towards markets and are more often positioned long than short. It is also important to note that small speculators in the commodity markets are less well capitalized than commercial interests, who generally take the opposite side of the trade (more about commercials in a later chapter). Because small speculators are not well capitalized, their focus, by necessity, is shorter term, and they frequently trail their sell stops below support (demand line of the triangle). Therefore, when this support level is breached, prices are likely to fall quickly as stops are set off in a chain reaction. The next rally is likely to lack power, as the majority of speculators will not be convinced of its validity until prices again achieve new highs.

While one could certainly choose to trade descending triangles as reversal patterns, this use of the pattern—to reverse a major uptrend—did not become part of the PPS Trading System. The descending triangle, when used to reverse a minor uptrend within a major downtrend, *did* become part of the system. This pattern is one of the "minor tops": a group of high-probability patterns used exclusively in downtrends. The following chapter explains exactly how to use these powerful patterns to exploit major downtrends.

Chapter 14

Minor Tops and Bottoms

> *A concept unique to PPS, the minor tops are essential when trading in downtrends. Learn how these patterns, which lack the power to reverse* major *uptrends, can effectively reverse minor *uptrends.*

Minor tops consist of three patterns: double tops, head-and-shoulders tops, and descending triangles. In PPS, these patterns are one of the primary ways we enter trades in *major downtrends.* You'll remember that the initial research considered these patterns a way to reverse a major uptrend. While they were shown to be only mildly effective when used that way, they are extremely effective when they are only required to reverse a minor uptrend within a major downtrend (see Figure 14–1).

While minor tops are quite prevalent in major downtrends, minor bottoms are extremely rare in major uptrends. This oddity is another example of the differing price behavior characteristics of uptrends and downtrends. In fact, so few minor bottoms were discovered that it was not possible to cull a statistically significant sample from the data. Abstracting from the sample, it was posited that double bottoms, when found in major uptrends, offer similar probabilities for success as double tops found in major downtrends.

Figure 14–1   **Minor Tops**

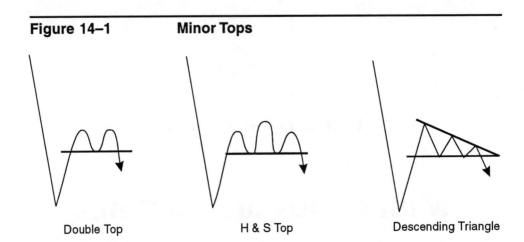

Double Top   H & S Top   Descending Triangle

Best Patterns ↑

Chapter   15

Rectangles and Wedges

> *Two patterns not previously discussed are examined within the context of uptrends and downtrends. Each of these important patterns will become part of the PPS Trading System.*

Rectangles

Defining the Pattern

Rectangles are congestion patterns bounded by horizontal lines on the top and bottom (see Figure 15–1). They form with a minimum

Figure 15–1   **Rectangle**

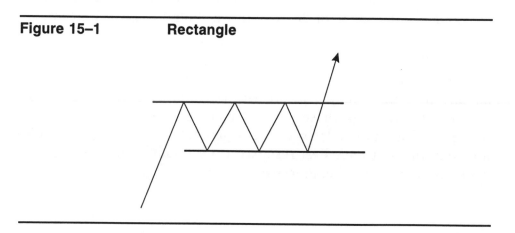

of four points; five to seven points are not unusual. Depending on the length of the congestion period and number of points, the rectangle may appear more square or elongated.

Methodology

Research was performed to determine whether shape made a difference, and also whether the number of points achieved during the construction was important. Rectangles found in uptrends were tested separately from those found in downtrends. Rectangles that reversed the underlying trend were tested separately from those whose formation acted as a continuation pattern. A final study was conducted to determine whether a rectangle would tend to reverse a trend or allow it to continue.

Results

Edwards and Magee stated that the rectangle is more often a consolidation pattern than a reversal pattern. My research confirmed their assumption. Four out of every five rectangles resolved themselves in the direction of the trend. Interestingly, the pattern was profitable regardless of whether it was tested as a continuation pattern or a reversal pattern. Traded as a continuation pattern, however, profits were three times as great. Overall, 47 percent of the trades were profitable. Traded as a reversal pattern, only 29 percent were profitable, while 52 percent were profitable traded as a continuation pattern.

Downtrends contained more rectangles: 59 percent versus 41 percent. In downtrends, three out of every four rectangles continued the trend; while in uptrends, a very high 86 percent continued the trend. No significant difference in profitability was found between uptrends and downtrends. Additionally, neither the number of points nor the shape of the pattern was found to be significant.

Conclusions

According to Edwards and Magee, rectangles are found less frequently in commodities and are less reliable. That statement may be correct. My research shows that rectangles act very much like triangles: They are indecision areas generally preceding the continuation of the trend. Best results can be obtained by trading the pattern only as a continuation pattern.

Rising Wedges

Defining the Pattern

The rising wedge is a five-point pattern. In one formed during an uptrend, there are two points on the demand line and three points on the supply line (see Figure 15–2). In the case of one formed during a downtrend, there are three points on the demand line and a minimum of two points on the supply line. In both instances, the important point to remember is that the supply and demand trend lines of the pattern must converge.

Of this pattern, Edwards and Magee said

> There is no evident barrier of supply to be vaulted but a gradual petering out of investment interest. Prices advance but each new wave of interest is feebler than the last. Finally demand fails entirely and the trend reverses. Thus a rising wedge typifies a situation which is growing progressively weaker in a technical sense...
>
> The difference between a rising wedge and what might be called a normal uptrend channel is that the wedge sets a sort of limit to the advance. Its converging boundary lines focus on a point near where the advance will halt and a reaction sets in.... Prices almost always fluctuate within the wedge's confines for at least two-thirds of the distance from the base to the apex; in many cases they rise clear to the apex, and in some they actually go a short distance beyond, pushing out at the top in a last gasp rally before collapsing. Once prices break out of the wedge downside they usually waste little time before declining in earnest. The ensuing drop ordinarily retraces all of the ground gained within the wedge itself, and sometimes more.

Figure 15–2   Rising Wedges Found in Uptrends and Downtrends

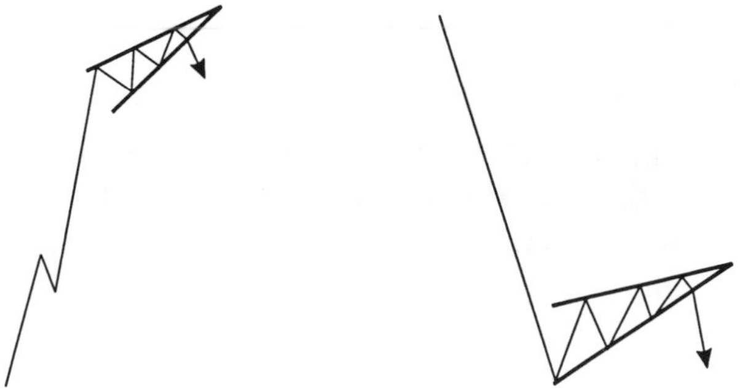

They also noted that the pattern ordinarily only reversed minor trends and at most, intermediate trends. They distinguished the rising wedge pattern from the pennant by requiring the wedge to form over a period of at least three weeks.

Methodology

There are two types of rising wedges. One type develops as a topping pattern after a previous uptrend; the second type starts at the bottom of a preceding downtrend. Each type was investigated separately. Also, several different strategies were tested on each rising wedge so as to elicit as much information from the pattern as possible.

Results

Rising wedges were found to be extremely rare. Because of the limited sample size, one should be cautious of the findings. Although several different strategies pertaining to stop placement were tried, the only successful one required that the stop be placed beyond the extreme point of the rising wedge. Using this strategy, however, rising wedges are too profitable to ignore. Those that occur after an uptrend are nearly twice as profitable as those that occur within a downtrend. If you have studied the Elliott Wave Theory, the former are what Elliott termed "diagonal fifth waves." My research results support his findings regarding the resolution of these patterns.

What are the practical applications of the rising wedge or "diagonal fifth"? One might assume that prices will decline to where the wedge began. Call that an objective, and assess risk/reward based on a stop placed beyond the extreme of the pattern (above the high). In cases where risk is too great, one could employ an option strategy. One final point to remember: The pattern is only likely to reverse a minor trend. If you are hoping for a major move, you must have more to go on.

Falling Wedges

Defining the Pattern

The falling wedge is a five-point pattern; if it forms during an uptrend, there are three points on the supply line and a minimum of two points on the demand line (see Figure 15–3). If formed during a downtrend, there are two points on the demand line and three

Figure 15–3   **Falling Wedges Found in**
                             Uptrends and Downtrends

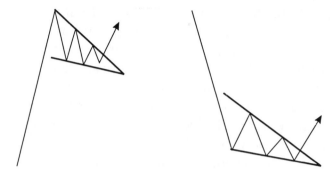

points on the supply line. Actually, the second or third point on the supply line may fall within the line formed by the other two points. The important thing to watch for is that three bottoms have formed. In many cases, the final bottom is only slightly below the previous one, causing the appearance of a double bottom at the bottom of the wedge.

Edwards and Magee distinguished between rising and falling wedges in terms of subsequent price action:

> Except for the fact that it is pointed down, the falling wedge appears in all respects like the rising form we have just described. But the price trend which follows its completion differs in character. When prices break out of a rising wedge they usually fall away rapidly, but when they move out of a falling wedge they are more apt to drift sidewise or in a dull "saucering-around" movement before they begin to rise. The rising wedge may, therefore, call for quick action to secure profits, while with a falling wedge the trader can ordinarily take his time about making his commitment for the ensuing rise.

Methodology

Falling wedges may also be classified as one of two types: The first type occurs after a previous uptrend and is a corrective pattern bounded by two converging lines. The second type appears after a downtrend, and is a reversal pattern bounded by two converging lines. Again, several different strategies were tested.

Results

Falling wedges were rare—though somewhat more prevalent than rising wedges. Still, the limited sample size should cause the trader to be cautious of the results. Beginning with uptrends, approximately two-thirds of the trades were profitable, and the profitability of the pattern was reasonably good. It appears that a trader would be justified in trading a falling wedge that occurs subsequent to an uptrend. Essentially, the pattern could be looked upon as a corrective pattern that temporarily has interrupted the uptrend. After the minor downtrend line (supply line) is breached, the trader should have good reason to get long in the direction of the trend. Unlike the case of the rising wedge, where the stop must be beyond the extreme of the pattern, the falling wedge is profitable not only when using that strategy, but when employing a tighter initial stop as well.

Falling wedges that occur in a downtrend are a different matter. It is difficult to know for sure when the falling wedge is complete. Often, the wedge will appear complete after a breakout has occurred; then prices will again test the low, sometimes breaking it and extending the wedge even further. Therefore, I cannot recommend the pattern when it occurs in a downtrend.

Chapter 16

Building the System

> *This chapter is packed with information you will need to trade PPS. Each pattern is compared, based upon its percentage of profitability and net profit per trade. Finally, those patterns with exceptional performance are selected to become part of PPS. A system chart makes it easy to remember which patterns to use in uptrends and downtrends.*

If you took the shortcut and skipped directly to this chapter, that's okay; but as time permits, you may want to go back and study the research on each of the various patterns examined in this section. For those of you who have slogged through what may have seemed like an endless inventory of dry statistics, congratulations on your effort. You now have a wealth of information about chart patterns and how to use them.

You should benefit from this in two ways: First, with the data as a constant source of reference, you may create any number of new systems on your own, varying the risk/reward, amount of trading activity, and any other factors to suit your own personal trading style. Second, by taking the time to study each of the patterns, you have made the research your own and will have more confidence in the system when you begin to trade it.

Building the system is as simple as combining the patterns that provide the most profitable risk reward/ratios. But before we attempt to do that, let's begin by looking at Table 16–1, which identifies each pattern, what percentage of trades were profitable, and the net profit per trade. **Note:** The net profit per trade is calculated not in dollars but in "units," which in and of themselves have no meaning other than to allow a comparison between the relative profitability of one pattern to another.

Table 16–1   Patterns—Profitability Table

Pattern	Percent Profitable	Net Profit per Trade
Ascending Triangle (uptrend)	43.2%	11.1
Ascending Triangle (downtrend)	20.0%	3.8
Symmetrical Triangle (with trend)	51.0%	21.2
Double Bottom	39.2%	6.7
Double Top (major uptrend)	28.0%	1.8
Double Top (minor uptrend)	54.5%	26.3
Descending Triangle (continuation)	18.0%	–3.7
Descending Triangle (reversal)	52.0%	10.0
Head-and-Shoulders Top	52.0%	2.3
Head-and-Shoulders Bottom	13.5%	–0.2
Triple Bottom	27.3%	5.2
Rectangle (continuation)	52.0%	16.0
Rectangle (reversal)	29.0%	5.1
Falling Wedge (uptrend)	50.0%	10.8
Falling Wedge (downtrend)	37.5%	5.2
Rising Wedge (uptrend)	100.0%*	22.3
Rising Wedge (downtrend)	37.5%	3.8

small sample size; not statistically significant

Qualifications

What qualifications make a pattern worthy of consideration for the system? First, the percentage of profitable trades must not be too low. Why? Because a long string of losses could occur, causing a severe drawdown. Of course, with a long-term trading system, we can't expect a high percentage of winning trades, and we need to be realistic. I decided to seek out patterns that would be profitable at least 40 percent of the time.

Next, we must be sure that the average trade shows a good profit. The net profit per trade tells us how profitable the pattern is. I decided to seek out patterns that would produce at least 10.0 units of profit per trade. Now let's review the chart to see how the system was constructed.

Starting with the **ascending triangle** found in an **uptrend,** we can see this is a powerful pattern that meets both our criteria. When we spot an ascending triangle in an uptrend, we'll trade it. We'll use the Bisected Angle Strategy to place our stop or overrule it with a fixed money management stop if it is too far away. We can expect the pattern to be more successful if found high up in the trend. We will ignore ascending triangles found in downtrends.

The **symmetrical triangle**, traded **with the trend**, also meets our criteria. In fact, the 21.2 unit net profit per trade shows this is an extremely powerful pattern. When we spot a symmetrical triangle, we will trade it in the direction of the trend, placing our stop at the apex. If the apex is too far away, we will overrule it with a fixed money management stop.

The double bottom meets neither of our criteria. Ignore it. The **double top** found in a major uptrend also fails our test. When found in a **minor uptrend within a major downtrend**, however, it takes on a different personality. The percentage of profitable trades is 54.5 percent, with a net profit per trade of 26.3 units. We will include it in our system. We will place our stop one-half the distance of the vertical height of the double top added to the neckline. If the risk is too great, we will revert to a fixed money management stop.

The **descending triangle** found in a downtrend does not merit our attention. However, we can trade it as a **reversal pattern of a minor uptrend** when found **within a major downtrend**. In this context, it is much like the double top, though its profit per trade is much less. We will use the Bisected Angle Strategy with the money management overlay.

The head-and-shoulders top does not warrant our consideration because of the low net profit per trade. Ditto for the head-and-shoulders bottom and triple bottom.

The **rectangle** does not offer much profit as a reversal pattern, but as a **continuation pattern**, it meets our criteria. We will place our stop one-half the distance of the height of the pattern or override that stop with a fixed money management stop if risk is too great.

In an **uptrend**, the **falling wedge** works well as a **continuation pattern** and fits our criteria. Placing the stop can be tricky depending on the size of the pattern. You may use a fixed money management stop. Another workable technique is to place the stop below the low of the breakout day. Depending on the slant of the wedge, a stop below the low of the pattern may be comfortable. Because this pattern is towards the low end of profitability, if you would rather be more conservative you may be justified in eliminating this pattern from the system. When markets in general are trending strongly—possibly due to major geopolitical events—the falling wedge can be used so that you will be more likely to catch those trends. Remember, in downtrends we do not trade the pattern because we have no way of knowing when the wedge will end.

The **rising wedge** found in an **uptrend** offers potential profits too impressive to ignore. The dropout of the wedge can be near vertical and offer spectacular profits in a matter of days. The reason, of course, is that most small speculators are long; any break in the market causes prices to avalanche through stops. This is one pattern whose potential you can be alerted to ahead of time: Ideally, you should see both open interest and volume decreasing as the pattern develops. That tells you that no fresh buying is coming into the market—unless a new fundamental emerges, the market is on borrowed time. Finally, an examination of internal market composition (the actual composition of open interest) may add to the evidence supporting an imminent price decline. A thorough discussion of internal market composition will be found in a later chapter. The stop is placed over the top of the rising wedge.

According to legend, a **rising wedge** found in a downtrend is a good trading pattern. But my research results do not agree—so I will ignore it. An exception would be if some kind of **topping formation** is observed at the top of the wedge. Then, the pattern may fall into the category of a reversal formation in a **minor uptrend within the context of a major downtrend.**

Summarizing the System

Our first task is to **determine whether the market is in an up-trend or downtrend** as indicated by the 40-day moving average. If an uptrend exists, we want to make sure it isn't weakening. Therefore, we will require the 18-day moving average to be rising as well. Remember, the 40-day moving average can be flat, as long as the 18-day moving average is rising.

Next, we will try to **spot one of the following patterns to go long:** symmetrical triangle, ascending triangle, rectangle, or falling wedge; in **uptrends,** we will also be alert for the potential formation of a rising wedge. If it's found, we will **look to outside confirmation** of internal market composition, open interest, and volume, rather than to moving averages.

If a **downtrend** exists, we expect to see the 40-day moving average either flat or declining, and the 18-day moving average declining. Then, we will attempt **to spot a symmetrical triangle to go short**. We will also be alert for minor countertrend rallies. If we find one that is topping as exhibited by a reversal formation such as a double top, descending triangle, or a small head-and-shoulders top, we will use the opportunity to go short. While such a case does not require an examination of the 18-day moving average, the 40-day moving average should be declining.

Table 16–2   **System Chart**

Uptrend Exists

Ways to Go Long	Ways to Go Short
1. Symmetrical triangle	1. Rising wedge
2. Ascending triangle	
3. Rectangle	
4. Falling wedge	

Downtrend Exists

Ways to Go Short	Ways to Go Long
1. Symmetrical triangle	None
2. Minor top (double top, descending triangle, head-and-shoulders top)	

Note: Before leaving this topic, you may at this time wish to refer to Appendix A and Appendix B, which offer even more detailed information on the research. Appendix A offers insights as to how the system performed in different market sectors. Appendix B examines the two strongest patterns over a 10-year period, comparing market-by-market performance.

Answers to Chartist's Quiz:

1. C	2. False	3. False	4. C	5. A
6. True	7. D	8. True	9. B	10. D

Additional Technical and Psychological Considerations

The three types of analysis presented here add another dimension to PPS—extending the methodology beyond simple chart mechanics. What you are about to learn you will find nowhere else; the techniques are based on original research. With this knowledge, you will have an understanding of futures markets that will put you on a level with even the most savvy professionals.

Chapter 17

Commitment of Traders

Learn why an understanding of open interest is crucial in futures trading. Are there really insiders in futures markets? And, if so, how can you benefit by examining their positions? You'll learn about my unique C.O.T. Index *and how I use it to find high-probability trades.*

"Open interest" denotes the number of outstanding long and short positions in a given market. It is more important, however, to know *who* holds these long or short positions. That statistic is tracked by the Commodity Futures Trading Commission, and is made available to the public every two weeks via a government publication known as the *Commitment of Traders Report.* Most wire services and even some chart services report the information. The report segregates open interest into three categories: commercials, large speculators, and small speculators.

In the stock market, the activity of insiders—defined as corporate officers, directors, and major shareholders—has long been recognized as a reliable indicator of future price movement. Even the scholarly efficient market hypothesis, which questions the use of fundamental and technical analysis, fully accepts the predictive value of insider activity. In futures markets, traders classified as "commercials" are indicators similar to the stock market's insiders.

Commercials

Commercials are those traders whose primary business is to produce or deal in the underlying physical commodity that they are also trading in the futures market. It is only reasonable to expect them to be more attuned to their commodity's future price prospects than someone outside the industry.

Commercials use the futures market to "hedge" or accept a known price now rather than risk an uncertain price at a future date. For example, a farmer may wish to lock in a price for his soybean crop months before his crop is actually harvested and brought to market. He sells "short" in the futures market to hedge his "long" physical position. By using the futures market, he can lock in a price now for his crop, eliminating the possibility that prices could drop lower before he gets his crop to the market. Depending on the farmer's outlook for future price prospects, he may only hedge part of his production. If prices rally in the months ahead, he may then increase his hedge, selling more contracts to lock in a higher average price.

Mining companies would follow the same procedure to hedge their future production; oil companies might do the same. In these cases, the type of commercial who uses the futures market in this way is known as a producer. But there is another type of commercial known as a processor. The processor needs to buy the final product that the commercial producer produces. For example, General Mills is a commercial processor that needs to buy wheat in order to make cereal. To eliminate the risk of future price increases, General Mills would buy wheat futures contracts. A maker of jewelry might do the same, using the silver or gold futures market to assure adequate raw materials at some future date. An oil refinery could buy futures contracts of crude oil so as to guarantee an adequate supply at a reasonable price.

You should understand that futures markets are *designed* for the purpose of allowing commercial interests to offset risk. Speculators offer the vehicle that allows them to do that. Speculators, by placing bets on future price movement, often take the other side of the trade: When the commercial sells contracts to hedge his physical position, he is often selling to a speculator who, thinking that prices will go higher, is buying futures contracts.

Before we leave the commercials, I should point out that in most commodity markets the producer utilizes the futures markets to a much greater degree than the processor. Therefore, when reference is made to commercials, we generally think of producers.

Speculators

Large Speculators

When a speculator trades a very large number of contracts, he is referred to as a large speculator. In most cases, large speculators are commodity funds. Though not always the case, technically oriented commodity funds typically follow trends in markets when strong trends exist. Going back to our example in which the soybean farmer would hedge his crop by selling futures when prices were rallying, normally the large speculator would be buying those contracts.

Small Speculators

The average individual trader falls into the category of small speculator. Ninety percent of the time, small speculators and large speculators are positioned similarly. In our soybean example, small speculators would likely be buying futures as well. Occasionally, when a market becomes quite oversold on a long-term basis, small speculators will perceive value and become buyers—even though a downtrend exists. But, for the most part, both large and small speculators are part of the same herd, often referred to just as speculators; their positions are usually opposite the commercials.

How to Use Commitment of Traders Data

An estimated 90 percent of all small speculators lose money trading futures. Theoretically, the futures market is a zero-sum game. That means that for every losing contract there is also a winning contract. (In point of fact, because of the cost of commissions and fees, it is actually not a zero-sum game. But for purposes of illustration, let's assume it is.) If 90 percent of small speculators lose money and their positions are generally opposite the commercials, it makes sense to think that commercials make most of the money in futures trading. That is the basic premise behind the theory.

W.O.W. Indexes

In 1982, long before the trading public had picked up on this idea, I launched a research project to try to determine whether one could make money by simply ascertaining how commercials were positioned in a particular market and then mimicking this "smart money." At the time, the report was little known in the brokerage and trading community. The one or two brokers I was able to find who had heard of it claimed it was worthless. When I received my copy, I could see why. Typical of a government publication, it was a maze of statistics printed in tiny type, with little explanation. But that didn't deter me.

I ordered all the prior monthly publications that I could find and began to build a database on every market. After months of tedious data entry, the database was finally complete. Then I was able to interrogate the database. A program was written to graph the positions of each of the three trader groups along with price data. When I examined the graphs, it was evident that when speculators held exceptionally large positions opposite that of the commercials, the market would often shortly thereafter embark on a sharp move favoring the commercials.

The reliability of this indicator was so great that we launched a monthly newsletter, *W.O.W Indexes* (Who Owns What), that depicted the current position of each of the three groups in each market along with my interpretation.

Commitment of Traders Index

A couple of years later, after leaving the research firm that acted as the publisher for that newsletter, I felt the *W.O.W. Indexes* still left much to be desired. One problem was that each market worked differently. In some markets, you never see the commercials net long, while in other markets commercials may be net long or net short to wide degrees. I knew I needed some way to analyze each market unto itself. It was then that I came up with the idea of normalizing the data.

Within each market, each group was examined and then *related* to prior data. For example, in the soybean market, commercials' net positions were first examined for every period during the previous four years. The most bullish net position over that period was given a score of 100; the most bearish net position registered was given a score of zero. Then the month's data was compared to that scale. The same was then done for large speculators and small speculators.

If the month's commercials' net positions were halfway between the highs and lows that had been experienced during the previous four years, the current reading would be 50 percent on the *Commitment of Traders Index*. A reading of 100 percent would mean that commercials were more bullish (according to their net positions) than at any time in the previous four years (regardless of whether they were net short). A reading of 0 percent would mean that commercials were more bearish than at any time during the previous four years. Large speculators and small speculators would each have a *C.O.T. Index* as well.

With all the information reduced to a single number, it was easy for me to spot significant imbalances that would often presage a major price move favoring the commercials. By comparing the current reading on the *C.O.T. Index* to the reading of the prior period, another important statistic was created. I called this the Movement Index. I found that a sudden move of significant magnitude in this index was nearly as significant as the reading on the *C.O.T Index*. Combined with an extreme reading on the *C.O.T. Index*, the two indices working in concert yielded even *greater* predictive value. For example, a reading of 92 percent preceded by a reading of 84 percent would have less predictive value than a reading of 92 percent preceded by a reading of 42 percent. In the latter case, the sudden jump in the Movement Index indicated that commercials were not only relatively bullish on the market as indicated by the *C.O.T. Index*, but had suddenly changed their outlook—as though privy to "inside information."

Shortcomings of Commitment of Trader Analysis

You can think of the *C.O.T. Index* as a sentiment indicator. When the crowd (speculators) are too bullish, it's a good time to sell; when the crowd is too bearish, it's a good time to buy. But as is the case with sentiment indicators in general, they cannot be used as timing indicators. Sentiment can remain at very high or very low levels for extended time periods. Let's go back to our original soybean example, and I'll explain why you can't bet the farm based on this indicator alone.

Soybean prices are rallying. If prices get over $8.00 a bushel, farmer Jones likes to start hedging his crop. He knows that in the spring prices sometimes rally if weather causes problems with plantings, and usually in the summer there is a good chance that hot or dry weather can cause another rally if it looks like the crop might be damaged. He also knows that if he doesn't sell some now and instead waits until harvest time, prices could be severely depressed as huge supplies come to market. The market keeps rallying to $10.00 a bushel; now farmer Jones is 50 percent hedged. That's about as far as he usually goes. The *C.O.T. Index* for commercials is now at 100 percent. Speculators are heavily long, hoping for a big bull market.

If you decide to fade the speculators based on the *C.O.T. Index*, here's what can happen. You sell short at $10.00. The weather continues hot, and the market goes to $11, $12, $13. You're getting murdered. But wait...you were supposed to be positioned short just like the smart money, the commercials. At $14 you cover your short positions and take a horrendous loss—$20,000 for every contract. Farmer Jones hedges the final 50 percent of his crop at $14. The market continues higher to $16. Is farmer Jones losing money? No way—he is hedged. No matter how much higher the futures market goes, he has the physical commodity to deliver when the time comes. His soybean crop is getting that much more valuable as prices go higher, offsetting the losses to his futures account.

It rains. The crop is saved. By harvest time, prices are back down to $7.00 per bushel. Farmer Jones sells his crop at an average price of $11.50 per bushel by using the futures market. Had you stayed short, you would have made $15,000 per contract. But there was no way you could take the risk of the market going any higher.

This example illustrates the difference between commercials and speculators: Commercials have deep pockets. They can generally withstand price movement adverse to their futures position, while the speculator *cannot*.

Another limitation of this form of analysis is that it works better in some markets than in others. Typically, the physical commodities are the best candidates, though very good results are also evident in the S&P, and especially in the bond market. In the currency markets, I have never found the analysis to be of much help. In those markets, the commercials are major money center banks. Most of their dealings are transacted in cash currency markets, so their positions in futures markets may not be reflective of their true overall positions.

How to Apply Commitment of Traders Analysis to the PPS Methodology

The *Commitment of Traders Index* is a wonderful indicator—if it's not abused. But it is only an *indicator*. It can tell you when internal market composition has reached an extreme imbalance, and that can forewarn you of a major price move favoring the commercials. But it can't tell you when to buy or sell or even where to place your stop. In isolation it is of little value.

When the PPS System began falling into place in 1987, my initial thoughts were that my theories on internal market composition would be of little value when trading PPS. That is because PPS is primarily a "with-trend" system. Remember, extremely high or low readings on the *C.O.T. Index*, which would presage a signal, always occur countertrend. For example, a reading of 100 percent on the index would indicate that commercials are more net long than at any time during the previous four years. This would normally occur after a prolonged downtrend. A reading of 0 percent on the index would mean that commercials are more net short than at any time during the previous four years and would normally occur after a prolonged uptrend.

In the normal course of things, given PPS's trend filters, PPS would generate only buy signals when the *C.O.T. Index* was approaching a reading that would turn the contrarian sentiment trader bearish. And vice versa in downtrends. But that is not *always* the case.

Again, expectations are for commercials to be buyers in downtrends and sellers in uptrends. Normally the opposite can be said for speculators who typically *follow* trends. But sometimes, something out of the ordinary happens, and the astute PPS student can put himself at great advantage. Sometimes I have watched markets move sideways to higher—price movement that would normally cause commercials to be sellers—only to see the *C.O.T. Index* marching dramatically higher. This happened in the copper market in 1988. For many weeks the market moved sideways to higher, while the *C.O.T. Index* readings for commercials continued to climb. Why? Commercials (insiders) knew something you and I didn't, and they wanted to cover their short positions at any cost, even if they had to pay higher prices. Soon thereafter, prices exploded. A nice symmetrical triangle issued a PPS buy signal, and I was on board one of the biggest trends of the year.

A more recent example occurred in the spring of 1993. Bonds had been in a long-term uptrend that stretched back over a decade; long-term interest rates hadn't been that low in longer than most traders could remember. You might remember the period. If you look back to newspaper articles in the spring of 1993, there was a flood of mortgage refinancings. The financial press warned that now was the time to refinance your home because rates would never be that low again; and the public bought into this notion, even in the futures market. Despite strong technical evidence that the major uptrend was still intact, the public turned bearish on bonds (see Figure 17–1). The *C.O.T. Index* reading for small speculators was 0 percent. They were more bearish than at any time during the previous four years. For large speculators, the reading was 12 percent, and for commercials the reading was 100 percent. In a decade of monitoring, I'd never seen readings that abnormal.

I vowed that this time if a PPS signal was generated I would *load the boat.* My reasoning was that if the market broke out to the upside, it would explode. Why? Speculators use stops. With all those short positions held by speculators, there had to be thousands of stops somewhere just over the highs. If a few were triggered, they would all catch like a brush fire in high winds.

So as to be sure not to miss the move, I dropped down a degree from the daily to an hourly chart. A triangle appeared, and I positioned long but this time with two-and-one-half times my normal size. Prices exploded as I knew they had to, catching small speculators and even major funds flatfooted. Those who tried to hold out just a few more days were punished for their stubbornness. Prices roared from 111 to 116 in just a month's time. Though not a major move by PPS standards, the extra-heavy position contributed to what turned out to be one of my biggest profits in 1993.

Both examples cited occurred when prices were in an uptrend. But you will find examples in downtrends also. In those cases, prices will be falling, but commercials, instead of buying, will be selling—as evidenced by a decline in the *C.O.T. Index.* You would then want to be more aggressive if you had the opportunity to establish a short position.

While opportunities of this kind don't come along frequently, among 30 different markets it would not be unusual to see two or three instances occur each year. Due to the extremely favorable odds the condition creates, it certainly makes sense to be able to recognize the situation when it appears. Thus, a correct analysis of Commitment of Traders data can benefit the PPS trader, and is considered part of the methodology.

Figure 17-1

C.O.T. Index Forecasts Major Price Rise

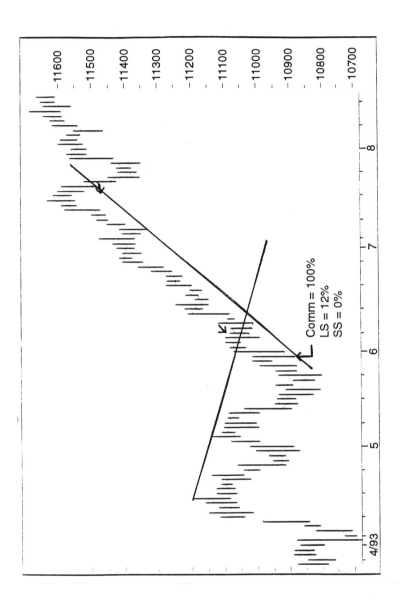

C h a p t e r   1 8

First Notice Days and Option Expirations

> Here is another chapter devoted to trading techniques derived entirely from original research. Learn the powerful effect that FNDs and Option Expirations exert on futures prices—and how to capitalize on that effect.

First Notice Days

Some commodity markets exhibit a feature called first notice day (FND). In those markets, if you are *long* futures contracts of the nearby month, you are required to either exit your position or roll forward to the next deferred contract on or before first notice day. Otherwise, the exchange assumes you want to take delivery of the contract (the actual physical commodity). Your brokerage firm knows that, as a speculator, that is not your intent. Therefore, if you forget to roll your position forward, they will typically notify you on or before that day. If you are *short* contracts in the delivery month, the first notice day rule does not apply. You are allowed to retain your short contracts up until the last trading day of the contract.

The average speculator is not aware of the effect of FND on price behavior. With the exception of what you are about to read, I have never seen published research on this important area of price behavior.

Let's start with a scenario: November soybeans, a popular month for the soybean contract, may be traded until November 18th, the last trading day. However, the FND is the last business day of the previous month—for our example, let's use October 31st.

By some estimates, the futures arena exhibits a 20 percent turnover rate each year, as new traders enter the market and old ones leave. If these estimates are accurate, tens of thousands of new traders, lacking experience and quite possibly unfamiliar with FND rules, are possible candidates for a role in the following drama.

Nicky Neophyte is long the nearby contract, totally oblivious to the fact that he must roll forward before October 31st. We will assume that his position is profitable, but that recently he has taken some hits in other markets. On October 30th, his broker calls to inform him that he must either roll forward to the January contract or liquidate the position. Nicky is on the golf course on his cellular phone, about ready to tee off. Having suffered a run of losses in other markets, he reasons that if he takes his profit now in the soybeans, his account will be at breakeven. Without additional consideration, he responds to his broker, "Just get me out." Dutifully, his broker enters an order to liquidate the position the following morning at the open.

Do you realize what just occurred? *Artificial* selling pressure came into the market. I refer to the selling pressure as artificial because it had nothing to do with technical or fundamental considerations. Normally, this effect is more pronounced if the market has been in a major uptrend. In that case, more speculators will be long and will be required to liquidate their positions in the nearby contract as required by the FND rule. This phenomenon could affect our trades. How can we know for sure? By performing research.

First Notice Day Research Study

Methodology

We first ran PPS Software, using 15 years of data, on seven major commodities that could be affected by first notice day. We then selected only those trades that were initiated during the 10-day period prior to FND. Finally, we compared the results of those trades to the results of trades initiated outside of the 10-day window. We also divided our sample into long and short trades, to determine whether the fact that the market was in an uptrend or a downtrend would have an impact on the results (see Tables 18–1 and 18–2).

Table 18–1	First Notice Day Study—Longs	
Market	***FND Trades*** **Percent Profitable**	***Others*** **Percent Profitable**
Soybeans	40%	36%
Corn	13%	36%
Wheat	0%	40%
T-Bonds	25%	39%
Gold	29%	25%
Cotton	31%	30%
Cocoa	29%	29%

Table 18–2	First Notice Day Study—Shorts	
Market	***FND Trades*** **Percent Profitable**	***Others*** **Percent Profitable**
Soybeans	43%	17%
Corn	44%	33%
Wheat	50%	39%
T-Bonds	27%	24%
Gold	24%	32%
Cotton	43%	28%
Cocoa	8%	49%

Results of First Notice Day Study

Examination of long trades revealed that three commodities displayed a statistically significant lower percentage of profitable trades, while none showed a statistically significant higher percentage. T-bonds, corn, and wheat produced significantly inferior results when trades were initiated in the 10-day period prior to FND. This tendency was so pronounced in corn and wheat that the trader would be well advised to avoid long trades in these markets during this critical period. In these two markets, only one out of 17 trades (5.9 percent) were profitable—compared to 26 out of 70 (37 percent) during normal times.

As to short trades, five out of seven markets tested demonstrated an abnormally higher percentage of winning trades initiated during the critical FND period. As was the case in the prior test on long trades, wheat again demonstrated the most sensitivity to this FND phenomenon.

Conclusions

In summary, it is clear that in those markets where FNDs exist, there is a sharp tendency for the market to suddenly pull back, if in an uptrend, and to accelerate to the downside if in a downtrend. Thus, the trader who spots a PPS pattern prompting him to go long may be well advised to wait until the artificial pressure caused by FND has passed before entering a position. On the other hand, if a PPS trader attempts to short a market that is in a downtrend, his odds of success are *increased* if he is able to enter during this critical period. It should be noted that this phenomenon was clear in Chicago Board of Trade markets, especially in the grains; yet it did not seem to be a factor in the New York markets that were tested.

Option Expirations

Some commodities offer options on the futures contract. For those that do, there is an option expiration date, which occurs well ahead of the last trading day for the contract and generally ahead of first notice day as well.

For some time, I have been aware of a market tendency regarding option expiration day. A test that examined PPS trades initiated within a 10-day window prior to option expiration days was conducted. Results were compared to trades initiated outside the window. However, the data sample of PPS trades was too small to draw statistically valid conclusions. Had the research study examined price behavior itself, rather than actual PPS trades, the data sample might have been adequate. (Most futures options did not start trading until 1985–1987.) So, while I can't offer you statistical proof of this phenomenon, I think that when I explain why it occurs you will agree that it makes sense.

A significant part of the futures brokerage industry is comprised of small brokerage firms whose primary business is to sell options. In the trade, these brokerage operations are known as boiler rooms. Most of the accounts opened by these firms are with customers who have never traded futures before and know practically nothing about it. The typical broker who works at these firms often knows very little about trading himself, but he is a first-rate salesman. He convinces the customer to open a small account, typically in the $5,000 range—though of course he will attempt to get as much as he can. His primary selling tool is the assertion that, unlike trading actual futures contracts, by purchasing options the customer always has a known risk. He can't possibly lose more than the price of the option.

The broker then plays up the potential for the customer to "triple his money in a couple of weeks" by getting on board a particular trend that is already in force. Usually, he is able to back up his claims with supporting articles from *The Wall Street Journal* or other investment publications. Often, in the case of weather, natural disasters, or major geopolitical events, the prospect may already be aware of the underlying fundamental news that has caused the trend.

After "educating" the prospect on the basics of how options work, he then convinces him to buy calls or puts on a particular market. More often, the customer buys calls. This is because speculators prefer the long side of markets and because the market that makes news is usually one whose price, due to a perceived shortage of supply, has climbed steadily.

Given that the broker has convinced the customer of the probability of further price increases and that the purchase of call options would make sense, the next decision to be made is what strike price will be purchased. The higher the strike price, the less likely it is that the price of the futures will reach that level before option expiration day. Therefore, options with higher strike prices will be priced more cheaply the further out of the money one goes. The broker, paid a commission for each option purchased, wants the customer to buy as many options as possible, and therefore recommends the lower-priced, far out-of-the-money "long shots." If the strike price is achieved, the customer could make as much as 10 times his initial investment. That sounds very appealing—especially given the fact the customer does not truly understand the odds against him.

If, as I have speculated, in a bull market there are thousands of unsuspecting call options sold to unsophisticated customers, then who sells the options to them? (For every buyer, there must be a seller.) The answer is that the sellers of these call options are floor brokers who make their living by doing just that. Without getting into a detailed explanation of option theory, which is beyond the scope of this book, I'll briefly explain how it works. In a bull market, option volatility increases and the premium expands on the option. The out-of-the-money options will tend to become overpriced—the premium is too expensive relative to the odds of success. The floor broker will sell these overpriced call options to the public, so as to pocket a rich premium. As long as the futures price of the underlying contract does not exceed the strike price of the option before the option expiration date, the floor broker will pocket the premium the customer pays for the right to buy the option. This, in fact, is what occurs 90 percent of the time.

The floor broker, however, is not going expose himself to unlimited risk should the market continue to skyrocket. He needs to protect himself. How does he do it? By buying futures contracts. Now he *can't* lose. If the market were to exceed the strike price, the profits from his long futures position would offset any losses on his short call position. But, of course, that does not usually happen. Instead, on option expiration day, the option will expire worthless. When it does, the floor broker will no longer need to hold the long futures contracts and will sell them. So, as is the case with FNDs, artificial selling pressure will come into the market. In this case, that will occur immediately after option expiration day.

In Figure 18–1, I have reproduced a chart of September 93 coffee. Look carefully at the early July period. Notice the huge up day that took prices above major resistance and closed at approximately 72.00. I would be willing to bet that *The Wall Street Journal* focused on this market the next day, citing bullish fundamentals. Can you imagine commodity brokers getting on the phone to recommend to their customers September call options with a strike price of 80.00? Notice how the price stopped just shy of the option

Figure 18–1

Option Expiration, Coffee, September 1993

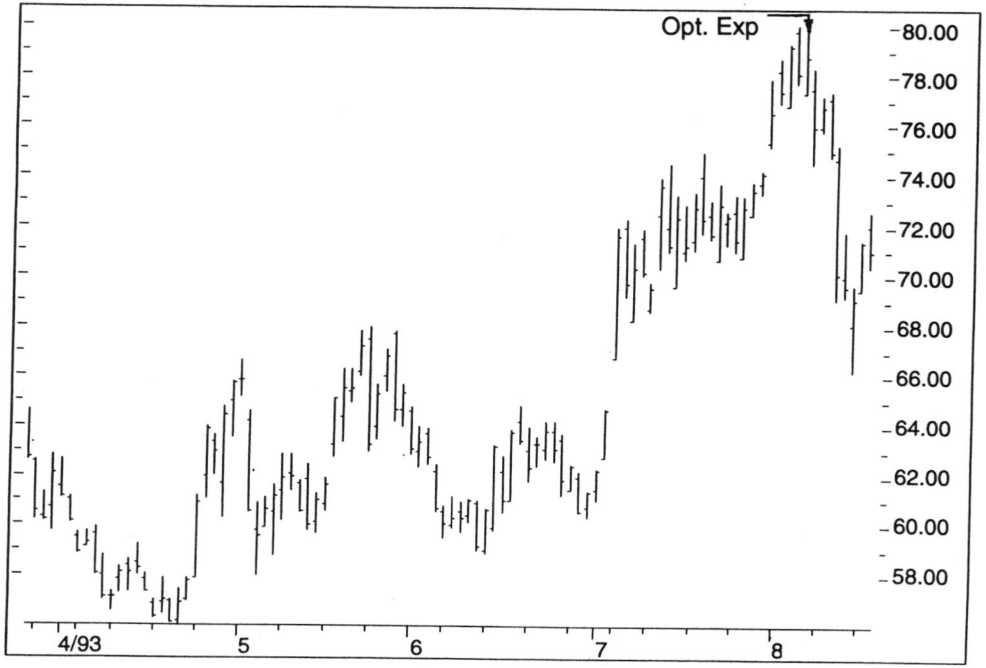

going in the money, and the day after option expiration, the price plunged.

In summary, we may use this knowledge to filter trades that may be signaled shortly before an option expiration date. We should wait until after option expiration selling pressure has subsided before attempting to establish long positions in an uptrend. Though the phenomenon may also present itself—in reverse—in downtrends to a lesser degree, I cannot substantiate that supposition.

Chapter 19

Basis and Spread Relationships

> *Futures contracts are priced according to expectations of a commodity's price at some time in the future. The true price of a commodity, on the other hand, is represented by what is referred to as the* cash or spot *price. A thorough understanding of basis and spread relationships will allow you to distinguish between a strong market whose futures price is rising due to real demand* for the commodity, *and a weak market whose futures price is rising as a result of pure* speculation.

Basis Relationships

Basis is the difference between the cash price of the commodity and the price in the futures market. Normally, for markets where commodities must be stored, the futures price of the nearby contract is above that of the cash (or "spot") price, and the deferred contracts are priced above the nearbys. That is to compensate for the cost of carrying the commodity in inventory—In other words, the cost of storing the commodity, plus insurance costs, plus an interest rate factor. A market priced this way is called *contango* and is the norm.

(Note—higher interest rates increase the carrying cost. The reasoning is that money could be put to better use in T-bills than in inventory.)

Sometimes, however, the demand for the commodity becomes so strong that the cash price of the commodity is higher than the nearby futures contract, and the nearbys are priced higher than the deferreds. A market priced this way is said to be in *backwardation* and is *not* the norm. The price structure reveals that the market is being driven by true demand, not just by speculation.

Consider how different market motivations would influence the price structure. A bull move that is *speculative* would put upward price pressure on deferred contracts because *speculators* would purchase *futures* contracts in *expectation* that prices will be higher at some point in the future. On the other hand, if true demand exists for the commodity—there is a real shortage, and processors must acquire the actual commodity now to meet demand for their products—the cash price (real price) would rise above the futures price (fictional price based on speculation).

Backwardation, by definition an indication that strong demand exists for a commodity, is typically associated with bull markets. Like bull markets, bear markets also are normally in a contango price structure. The fact that the cash price is below the futures price infers that no strong demand exists for the actual commodity; in all likelihood prices will continue to work lower.

A word of caution: While the contango price structure is the norm for physical commodity markets, the degree of the basis may be important. An accurate assessment would require a separate analysis of each market to determine a normal basis in that commodity. Remember, each commodity will have its own cost to carry, and the interest rate is constantly varying. In addition, you must remember that the basis (the difference between the cash price and the price of a particular futures contract) will shrink each day as the future comes ever closer to the present. An illustration may clarify that concept. In a contango market, on March 15th the price of July soybeans may be 30 cents higher than the cash price. But as the expiration of the July contract approaches, the futures price and cash price will come ever closer together until, on the day that the July contract expires, they become the same.

Spread Relationships

Understanding and correctly using basis relationships is a complex and difficult task. Fortunately, we can derive basically the same information—that is, whether there is true demand for the commodity or just speculative interest—by observing spread relationships between nearby and deferred futures contracts. And, in fact, that is what most analysts do.

Using soybeans again as an illustration, assume that it is March 15th. If true demand asserts itself in the market, it will be reflected in the May/July spread, which will increase in value. A market in backwardation would normally invert the entire price structure: The cash market would be priced above nearby futures contracts, and nearbys would be priced above the deferreds.

Depending on the market and the particular delivery months of the futures contracts, you may want to monitor more than one spread. For example, in February, you might want to look at the March/May, March/July, and May/July spreads. Unlike basis, the convenient aspect of spreads is that the differential is not affected by the convergence of the future and the present; the time between the May futures contract and the July futures contract is a fixed quantity.

How to Use Spread Relationships in Your Trading

Often, major bull moves are telegraphed in advance by spread relationships: The nearby futures contract will make sharp gains on the deferred contracts, and the market may go into backwardation. When that occurs, you should look for an opportunity to position long and be aggressive in your buying. The market is in strong hands and is moving higher because of true demand. As prices advance, speculative interests may join the fray and exert even more upward pressure on prices.

Figure 19–1 illustrates that very phenomenon. The three charts are of March KW (Kansas City wheat), May KW, and the March/May spread. In September, notice how the March contract, already at a premium, began advancing sharply on the May contract. This occurred well before the bulk of the bull move, which at

Figure 19–1   **Spread Relationship**
                       Indicating Backwardation

Wheat 94 March KW

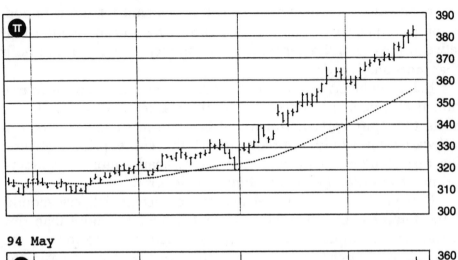

94 May

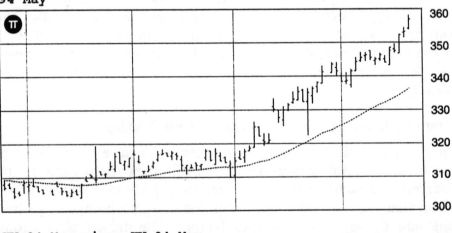

KW 94 Mar minus KW 94 May

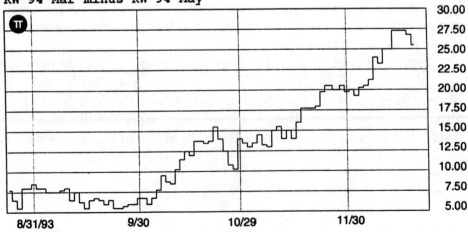

the time was still in its embryonic stage. The astute PPS trader would have used this knowledge to his advantage.

The use of basis and spread relationships as I have detailed them is only applicable in physical commodities. In financial markets—and most observably in interest rate markets—the phenomenon is reversed. If commercials expect higher interest rates in the future, their expectation is that the *instrument* (for example, T-bonds or Eurodollars) will be priced lower in the future. Thus, as an accurate reflection of their sentiment, the deferred contracts will be priced considerably lower than the nearby contract.

Chapter 20

Mental Hurdles

Learning a profitable approach to trading would be of little value if the trader were not prepared mentally for the battle that lies ahead. This chapter will explain why system trading is so difficult and how you must think in order to be successful at it.

If you are relatively new to commodity trading, chances are you will underestimate the importance of the psychological aspects of the game. After all, it certainly seems easy enough: Buy when your system says to buy, and sell when your system says to sell. However, if you were to ask any professional trader what the most difficult part of trading is, he would tell you it is dealing with the psychological aspects. Put another way, it is not allowing your emotions to interfere with your trading.

Let's examine some typical ways in which your emotions *could* affect your trading. We will assume you have a set of rules that guide you in your decision making and that you are not simply trading by the seat of your pants. Your rules tell you when to get into a market, how much to risk, and when to get out of a market. Here we go.

Case #1. You went short crude oil yesterday because it appears to be in a downtrend, and your system gave a signal. You place a stop 50 cents from your entry, risking $500. So far, the market is trading about where you went short. On the evening news, you hear that one of the OPEC ministers is planning to ask fellow OPEC members to cut production at next week's meeting.

The next morning, the price of crude is 35 cents higher, and you are holding a $350 loss. You assume the market will continue higher, so you cover your position and accept the $350 loss. An hour later, the market is 45 cents higher than where you first entered; you pat yourself on the back for cutting your losses. Then, a news flash suggests that the OPEC rumor was completely unfounded. Prices plummet. Two weeks later prices are $3.00 lower. You should have made $3,000—instead, you *lost* $350.

Case #2. You have just suffered eight losing trades in a row. Your total losses exceed $4,000. Fortunately, you are long the T-bonds, and they have been going straight up for the last two weeks. You bought them at 90.00, and they are now trading at 94.04. You have a little over $4,000 in open profit. You reason that the market is overdue for a correction. Not wanting to risk giving back your open profit, you liquidate your position.

T-bond prices continue higher over the next several days. Soon they are trading at 96.16, and the news is very bullish. You kick yourself for getting out too soon and are determined not to let any more of the move get away from you. You buy, despite not having a good place for a stop.

The market starts to drop. You can't believe it. You realize you have not put in a stop. "It's only a correction," you tell yourself. "The market deserves a little correction. If I get out, I might not be able to get back in."

The correction turns into a rout. In only a couple of days, you have lost more than $2,000. You're shell-shocked. "How could this be happening to me?" you cry. "Please, God, just let me get back to breakeven and I promise never to do something stupid like that again." Your plea falls upon deaf ears. Cursing the irrationality of the market, you eventually liquidate, taking a $2,500 loss. Had you followed your system to the letter, you would have finished the month with a $1,200 gain.

These two cases are typical, but in no way all-inclusive of the myriad ways in which the markets can influence you to deviate from your established trading plan. Despite having a trading plan, the average trader is not immune to outside factors, assuming that some authority knows more than he does about the imminent direction of prices. You must steel yourself against these external influences and follow your rules to the letter. Having a trading plan is of no use if you don't *follow* it.

Over 10 years ago, a large number of seminar attendees paid thousands of dollars to learn a trading system taught by a well-known trader. One year after the seminar, third-party monitoring showed the system had performed extremely well; yet, incredibly, a survey of those attendees showed that less than 10 percent were still using the system only one year later.

Those statistics do not surprise me. As I pointed out in Chapter 2, most traders lose because they lack consistency. Their losses result not from a lack of analytical ability, but rather from a lack of personal trading discipline. So why *is* it so difficult to stick with a trading system?

Why System Trading Is So Difficult

When we hold our PPS Advanced Training seminars, we often invite Mark Douglas, author of *The Disciplined Trader,* to teach our PPS students personal trading discipline so that they will be more successful with PPS. I have never seen the reasons why system trading is so difficult expressed better than in Mark's book, and so, with his permission, I quote from it here.[*]

> Trying to outguess your trading system is an exercise in extreme frustration. Sometimes the system will give you signals to trade in ways that are completely contrary to your logic and reasoning. Sometimes the system will defy your reasoning and be right, and sometimes you will agree with the system and it will be wrong. You need to understand that technical trading systems are not designed to be outguessed. What I mean is, they aren't designed to give you isolated signals of an opportunity to be taken when it seems right. What they do is mathematically define, quantify and categorize past relationships in collec-

---

[*] Reprinted by permission from Mark Douglas, *The Disciplined Trader: Developing Winning Attitudes* (New York: New York Institute of Finance/Simon & Schuster, pp. 211–213). For further information, the author can be contacted at Trading Behavior Dynamics, Inc. (312) 938-1441.

tive human behavior to give you a statistical probable outcome of the future.

As a comparison to trading, it is much easier to take risks and participate in a gambling event with a purely random outcome based on statistical probabilities, simply because it is random. What I mean is, if you risk your money on a gambling event that you know has a random outcome, then there's no rational way you could have predicted what that outcome would be. Therefore, you don't have to take responsibility for the outcome if it isn't positive.

Whereas, with trading, the future is not random. Price movement, opportunity, and outcomes are created by traders acting on their beliefs and expectations of the future. Every trader contributes to the outcome of the future by putting on and taking off trades in accordance with their beliefs. Because traders actually create the future by collectively acting on their beliefs about the future, the outcome of their actions is not exactly random. Why else would traders try to outguess their systems, unless they had some concept of the future and how that future will affect the markets?

This adds an element of responsibility to trading that doesn't exist with a purely random event and that is difficult to avoid. This higher degree of responsibility means that more of your self-esteem is at stake, making it much more difficult to participate. Trading gives you all kinds of ways to beat yourself up for all the things you should have or could have considered that would have resulted in a more satisfying outcome.

Furthermore, you don't trade in an information vacuum. You form your expectations about the future with information technical systems don't take into consideration. Consequently, this sets up a conflict between what your intellect says should be happening and the purely mathematical means of predicting human behavior afforded by your technical system. This is precisely why technical systems are so difficult to relate to and execute. People aren't taught to think in terms of probabilities—and we certainly don't grow up constructing a conceptual framework that correlates a prediction of mass human behavior in statistical odds by means of a mathematical formula.

To be able to execute your trading systems properly, you will need to incorporate two concepts into your mental framework—thinking in terms of probabilities and correlating the numbers or the mechanics of your system to the behavior. Unfortunately, the only way you can really learn things is actually to experience them by executing your system. The problem is that rarely will the typical trader stay with his system beyond two or three losses in a row, and taking two or three losses in a row is a very common occurrence for most trading systems. This creates something of a paradox or Catch-22. How do you do it if you don't believe it? And, you won't learn to believe it unless you do it long enough for it to become a part of your mental framework. This is where you employ mental discipline to make flawless execution a habit.

Personal Trading Discipline and PPS

Although PPS is undeniably one of the most profitable trading systems ever developed, I would be the last to argue that trading PPS is easy. It demands from the trader patience and fortitude, and a commitment the average trader is not willing to make. Paradoxically, the very elements of PPS that are responsible for its success are also responsible for testing the personal discipline of the PPS trader.

PPS is an intermediate- to long-term trading system and requires a matching perspective; success can not be expected within a few months. The average commodity trader, short term in his orientation, will not stay with a system for that amount of time if he is not making money.

PPS employs one algorithm that limits initial risk and another that causes the stop to be moved to breakeven quickly. Those techniques, while protecting capital, also ensure that the majority of PPS trades will result in losses or break-even trades. And, as Mark Douglas pointed out, many traders are simply not prepared to accept a string of losing trades.

It is not uncommon for PPS to make the majority of its profit in a given year from just three trades. Yet the trader may need to enter 125 trades to find those three big winners. Generally, small- to medium-sized winning trades offset the large number of small losses, while the few big winning trades put the PPS trader over the top. While it is possible to find those big winning trades evenly dispersed throughout the course of the year, it is equally common to find them bunched into one quarter; so the trader may have to wait as long as nine months before seeing any improvement to his bottom line.

None of the mental hurdles placed before the PPS trader is insurmountable, however. The trader must simply come into the game adequately capitalized and with a full realization that he will need to withstand drawdowns and go through periods when he will not make money. *If, and only if,* the trader is willing to accept those conditions, can he expect to become successful with PPS.

PPS Software and Portfolio Analyzer

If you do not own a personal computer, you may wish to skip the first chapter of this section, which details the design of PPS Software. The remaining three chapters, however, will be relevant to all. You'll learn how to create a winning portfolio and how to compound your returns more rapidly through the application of fixed-fractional money management techniques.

Chapter 21

PPS Software Design

PPS was first computerized in 1992. If you are interested in using PPS Software or in writing your own programs for trading, you will find this chapter informative.

In 1991, we embarked on a massive undertaking: translating the PPS methodology into computer code. Fifteen thousand lines of code and almost a year later, we released the first version of PPS Software. Two questions arose: 1) How does PPS Software compare to the original methodology in terms of performance? and 2) How accurately does the software reflect the original methodology?

In answer to the first question, let me say that before beginning to trade PPS myself in 1988, I had compiled 10 years of performance data on 18 different markets. Over the 10-year period, no market lost money, and there was never a losing year. That performance data, manually produced, is what gave me the confidence to begin trading PPS. Our first pass at computerizing PPS showed historical results very close to those manual results. At that point, we knew that the mathematical algorithms had captured the essence of the original PPS methodology.

The question as to which performs better, software or manual methodology, is one that can't be answered by looking at numbers alone, however. Remember, my original tests were performed manually, in hindsight. It is one thing to paper trade the past; it is something else to trade a system in real time. Also, although the rules of the methodology are quite clear, there is certainly a degree of judgment and a skill factor involved; some traders will simply have more aptitude for pattern recognition than others.

Further, even given similar skill factors, any two traders' results could vary radically over the short term. For example, in drawing a trend line, the thickness of a pencil width could represent a tick. Assume two traders are in a trade. A trend line is drawn and stops are placed. Trader A's stop is one tick further away than trader B's. Trader B is stopped out, but trader A remains in the trade—one that turns out to be a huge winner. I have actually seen this occur more than once.

The commercial release of the PPS software was well received. It appealed to two trading segments that were reticent to commit to a methodology. The first group consisted of what I will call the "scientific" type. This type of trader, often from an engineering or computer background, insists on hard data from the computer. He wants to see a mathematical exactness in the trading logic and needs the ability to historically test a system on his computer. His rigorousness is to be applauded. However, having personally witnessed the trading education of hundreds of these types of traders, I can unequivocally state that they are often their own worst enemy. Their attention to detail is such that they often fail to appreciate that markets are more than just numbers. There is a lot to know about markets that can only be learned from *trading them*. Most importantly, markets change. Markets can and will behave in unprecedented fashions. Historical testing, while a valuable tool, has certain limitations and is only a beginning point for the successful trader.

The second group of traders who eagerly embraced the software were those traders who simply did not want to put in the time and effort required to learn the methodology, but wanted to be spoon-fed winning trades just as quickly as their computers could spit them out. These traders are just one step removed from those who rely solely on hotlines and newsletters for their trading advice. Fortunately, our educational efforts have convinced most of our customers that it is worth the time and effort to learn the complete methodology.

What the Software Does

Getting back to the second question—how well the software reflects the original methodology—I will first explain in basic terms what the software does and then address its limitations with regard to the original methodology. Let's assume that we have a market where an uptrend appears underway. Immediately, there is a discrepancy between the methodology and the software. Whereas the methodology employs both a 40-day and an 18-day moving average to determine the trend, the software employs only a 28-day moving average, validating a long signal by requiring that the point of entry lie above it, the reverse for a short signal. Which approach works better? Historical testing shows no significant difference. Many students place too much emphasis on these moving averages. There are no magic numbers; they are simply guidelines.

Now that the computer has spotted a market that is moving smartly upwards, it begins to monitor what we will call the "thrust." Once certain mathematical qualifications related to movement per unit of time are met, the computer recognizes that a thrust has occurred and shifts into another mode. In this mode, the computer is watching and waiting for a price reaction to occur. Any pullback is then monitored until certain qualifications are met, allowing the "reaction" to be labeled as such.

In the next mode, the computer looks for a "test" of the original thrust. Once a test has occurred, the computer once again looks for a reaction. When a thrust, reaction, test, and reaction have been identified, the computer draws a trend line from the high point of the thrust to the high point of the test. The system will enter a trade one tick above that trend line if that price is above the 28-day moving average. Signals to go short work in reverse.

When markets trend, they tend to move higher in a series of thrusts followed by consolidations. Therefore, if a market is trending, a signal is likely. The mathematical algorithm, while not distinguishing between patterns, tends to recognize patterns that look like symmetrical triangles, ascending triangles, rectangles, and falling wedges. Because the computer is bound by precise rules relating to vertical (price) movement and horizontal (time) movement, occasionally it will miss patterns that, visually, appear tradeable. Conversely, at other times, its mathematical requirements will be satisfied by patterns that might not be readily visible.

What the Software Does Not Include

Once the software has signaled a trade, it will not look for another entry signal. In the methodology, once the stop has been raised to breakeven or better, a second position is allowed if a new signal occurs. A lighter position (fewer contracts) is recommended. If a trend continues for some time, the advantage of having a second position on is quite obvious. In recent years, however, there have been fewer opportunities to pyramid (add additional contracts). Still, the trained PPS trader may benefit by monitoring a profitable open position, in hope of adding a second position should the opportunity occur.

In the area of trend identification, the software is not highly discriminatory. Using the 28-day moving average, it will prevent the trader from attempting to buy in an established downtrend or sell in an established uptrend. But the 28-day moving average alone is not enough to assure that a strong trend is underway. There have been times when I've seen a market move sideways in congestion for so long that the 28-day moving average has flattened to a nearly horizontal line. In such cases, signals could be generated either long or short while the market remained in congestion. While I would not take these signals, it would be valid to argue that all system signals should be taken. Although these signals may exhibit a lower probability, any particular signal could be extremely profitable.

The software does not distinguish among signals of varying quality. You might remember that each individual pattern exhibits a unique probability. That is, individual patterns exhibit varying success rates depending upon where they are found in a trend. For example, ascending triangles have a much higher probability of success when found higher in the trend.

The software does not take into account the "additional technical considerations"—such as open interest considerations exhibited by the *Commitment of Traders Index*, basis relationships, or the effect of first notice days and option expirations. If it did, the number of trades would be reduced significantly, and the results of historical testing would be suspect. Adding more variables takes us in the direction of overoptimization. For a system to remain robust—and by that I mean it exhibits the greatest likelihood that future results will be similar to historical results—it should be designed with as few parameter variables as possible.

How PPS Software Works

In order to run PPS Software, you must subscribe to a futures database. Since PPS runs on daily data, you only need to pick up data via modem once a day; end-of-day data is relatively inexpensive. Some historical data are required as well. PPS requires at least four months of data to correctly make calculations. Ideally, you will want to buy a historical database of at least five and preferably 10 years, so that you can perform historical testing. At the time of this writing, PPS is compatible with the data formats of CSI and Technical Tools, two of the largest suppliers of futures data in the country.

PPS asks you the location (directory) where your data files reside, then addresses those files. You then select which markets you would like to trade and designate the specific contract—for example, July 95 Soybeans. After your portfolio is created, you can run a historical test or generate signals for the next day.

Four different reports are available: 1) The Daily Trade Signals Report lists details on current positions and the recommended trades for the next trading day (see Figure 21–1); 2) The Open Trades Report summarizes information on open trades (see Figure 21–2); 3) Today's Trades Report lists pertinent information concerning each position that was entered and/or exited during the most recent trading day (see Figure 21–3); and 4) The New Signals Report summarizes the new signals for the next trading day (see Figure 21–4).

Historical Testing

In order to perform historical testing quickly, you will want to create what is known as "continuous" data contracts. These contracts link the price data so there are not price discrepancies between successive contract months. A utility program to accomplish this may be available from your data vendor or can be purchased separately.

There are two modules in PPS Software: signals and optimization. *Signals* is the module that produces your signals for the next day. *Optimization* is the module that performs historical testing. In that mode, two reports are available: 1) The Performance Summary Report allows multiple reports to be created, one for each tested combination of PPS parameter variables (more about PPS parameter variables later; see Figure 21–5); 2) The Historical Trade Listing displays a trade-by-trade listing, even designating the rule that was used to generate both the entry and exit (see Figure 21–6).

Figure 21–1   **Daily Trade Signals Report**

```
---> P A T T E R N    P R O B A B I L I T Y    S T R A T E G Y   <---

                    Daily Trade Signals Report

            Signals generated 12-27-1994 for trading on 12-28-1994

US_MAR95--->>>   Current Position: LONG     Entry Date/Price: 941202    97^30
     --->>>   Exit Signal:  Sell Stop at:    99^09
     --->>>>>EXIT TODAY on the CLOSE [SELL MOC] IF:
             (1) The CLOSE is within the LOWER ONE FOURTH of the DAY's
                 ADJUSTED PRICE RANGE (TRUE High - ACTUAL Low)
             (2) The TRUE PRICE RANGE (TRUE High - TRUE Low) is
                 GREATER THAN:    1^28
             (3) The CLOSE is LESS THAN:  100^21
             (4) AND AT LEAST ONE of these two conditions is TRUE
             (4A) TODAY's TRUE PRICE RANGE is GREATER THAN:    1^10
             (4B) TODAY's LOW is LESS THAN:   99^26

TY_MAR95--->>>   Current Position: FLAT     Entry Date/Price: ------ -------
     --->>>   NO TRADE SIGNALS AT THIS TIME  <<<---

MB_MAR95--->>>   Current Position: LONG     Entry Date/Price: 941223    85^04
     --->>>   Exit Signal:  Sell Stop at:    85^04
     --->>>>>EXIT TODAY on the CLOSE [SELL MOC] IF:
             (1) The CLOSE is within the LOWER ONE FOURTH of the DAY's
                 ADJUSTED PRICE RANGE (TRUE High - ACTUAL Low)
             (2) The TRUE PRICE RANGE (TRUE High - TRUE Low) is
                 GREATER THAN:    2^04
             (3) The CLOSE is LESS THAN:   86^01
             (4) AND AT LEAST ONE of these two conditions is TRUE
             (4A) TODAY's TRUE PRICE RANGE is GREATER THAN:    1^15
             (4B) TODAY's LOW is LESS THAN:   85^08

ED_MAR95--->>>   Current Position: SHORT    Entry Date/Price: 941222    92.91
     --->>>   Exit Signal:  Buy Stop at:    92.95
     --->>>>>EXIT TODAY on the CLOSE [BUY MOC] IF:
             (1) The CLOSE is within the UPPER ONE FOURTH of the DAY's
                 ADJUSTED PRICE RANGE (ACTUAL High - TRUE Low)
             (2) The TRUE PRICE RANGE (TRUE High - TRUE Low) is
                 GREATER THAN:    .33
             (3) The CLOSE is GREATER THAN:   92.81
             (4) AND AT LEAST ONE of these two conditions is TRUE
             (4A) TODAY's TRUE PRICE RANGE is GREATER THAN:    .10
             (4B) TODAY's HIGH is GREATER THAN:   92.86

SF_MAR95--->>>   Current Position: FLAT     Entry Date/Price: ------ -------
     --->>>   NO TRADE SIGNALS AT THIS TIME  <<<---

DM_MAR95--->>>   Current Position: FLAT     Entry Date/Price: ------ -------
     --->>>   NO TRADE SIGNALS AT THIS TIME  <<<---

BP_MAR95--->>>   Current Position: FLAT     Entry Date/Price: ------ -------
     --->>>   NO TRADE SIGNALS AT THIS TIME  <<<---

JY_MAR95--->>>   Current Position: SHORT    Entry Date/Price: 941125   102.36
     --->>>   Exit Signal:  Buy Stop at:   100.85
     --->>>>>EXIT TODAY on the CLOSE [BUY MOC] IF:
             (1) The CLOSE is within the UPPER ONE FOURTH of the DAY's
                 ADJUSTED PRICE RANGE (ACTUAL High - TRUE Low)
             (2) The TRUE PRICE RANGE (TRUE High - TRUE Low) is
```

Figure 21-1   Daily Trade Signals Report (continued)

```
                    GREATER THAN:    1.17
                    (3) The CLOSE is GREATER THAN:   100.49
                    (4) AND AT LEAST ONE of these two conditions is TRUE
                    (4A) TODAY's TRUE PRICE RANGE is GREATER THAN:    .58
                    (4B) TODAY's HIGH is GREATER THAN:  100.75

CD_MAR95--->>>   Current Position: SHORT    Entry Date/Price: 941115    73.56
        --->>>   Exit Signal: Buy  Stop at:    72.09
        --->>>>>EXIT TODAY on the CLOSE [BUY MOC] IF:
                    (1) The CLOSE is within the UPPER ONE FOURTH of the DAY's
                        ADJUSTED PRICE RANGE (ACTUAL High - TRUE Low)
                    (2) The TRUE PRICE RANGE (TRUE High - TRUE Low) is
                        GREATER THAN:    .60
                    (3) The CLOSE is GREATER THAN:    71.33
                    (4) AND AT LEAST ONE of these two conditions is TRUE
                    (4A) TODAY's TRUE PRICE RANGE is GREATER THAN:    .14
                    (4B) TODAY's HIGH is GREATER THAN:    71.41

DX_MAR95--->>>   Current Position: FLAT    Entry Date/Price: ------ -------
        --->>>   NO TRADE SIGNALS AT THIS TIME  <<<---

GC_FEB95--->>>   Current Position: SHORT    Entry Date/Price: 941223    382.1
        --->>>   Exit Signal: Buy  Stop at:    384.4
        --->>>>>EXIT TODAY on the CLOSE [BUY MOC] IF:
                    (1) The CLOSE is within the UPPER ONE FOURTH of the DAY's
                        ADJUSTED PRICE RANGE (ACTUAL High - TRUE Low)
                    (2) The TRUE PRICE RANGE (TRUE High - TRUE Low) is
                        GREATER THAN:    5.2
                    (3) The CLOSE is GREATER THAN:    383.3
                    (4) AND AT LEAST ONE of these two conditions is TRUE
                    (4A) TODAY's TRUE PRICE RANGE is GREATER THAN:    1.8
                    (4B) TODAY's HIGH is GREATER THAN:    383.5

SI_MAR95--->>>   Current Position: SHORT    Entry Date/Price: 941221    482.5
        --->>>   Exit Signal: Buy  Stop at:    490.5
        --->>>>>EXIT TODAY on the CLOSE [BUY MOC] IF:
                    (1) The CLOSE is within the UPPER ONE FOURTH of the DAY's
                        ADJUSTED PRICE RANGE (ACTUAL High - TRUE Low)
                    (2) The TRUE PRICE RANGE (TRUE High - TRUE Low) is
                        GREATER THAN:    24.0
                    (3) The CLOSE is GREATER THAN:    482.5
                    (4) AND AT LEAST ONE of these two conditions is TRUE
                    (4A) TODAY's TRUE PRICE RANGE is GREATER THAN:    4.0
                    (4B) TODAY's HIGH is GREATER THAN:    483.5

PL_APR95--->>>   Current Position: FLAT    Entry Date/Price: ------ -------
        --->>>   NO TRADE SIGNALS AT THIS TIME  <<<---

HG_MAR95--->>>   Current Position: FLAT    Entry Date/Price: ------ -------
        --->>>   Buy Signal: Buy Stop at:   136.00  LIMIT:   140.05
        --->>>>>EXIT on DAY of ENTRY [SELL MOC] IF:
                    (1) The CLOSE is within the LOWER ONE FOURTH of the DAY's
                        ACTUAL PRICE RANGE (ACTUAL High - ACTUAL Low)
                    (2) AND AT LEAST ONE of these two conditions is TRUE
                    (2A) The CLOSE is LESS THAN:  135.90
                    (2B) TODAY's ACTUAL PRICE RANGE is GREATER THAN:    4.15

KC_MAR95--->>>   Current Position: FLAT    Entry Date/Price: ------ -------
        --->>>   NO TRADE SIGNALS AT THIS TIME  <<<---
```

Figure 21–1   Daily Trade Signals Report (continued)

```
CC_MAR95--->>>  Current Position: FLAT     Entry Date/Price: ------ -------
         --->>>  NO TRADE SIGNALS AT THIS TIME   <<<---

OJ_MAR95--->>>  Current Position: FLAT     Entry Date/Price: ------ -------
         --->>>  NO TRADE SIGNALS AT THIS TIME   <<<---

C__MAR95--->>>  Current Position: LONG     Entry Date/Price: 941223    231^4
         --->>>  Exit Signal: Sell Stop at:   229^0
         --->>>>>EXIT TODAY on the CLOSE [SELL MOC] IF:
                 (1) The CLOSE is within the LOWER ONE FOURTH of the DAY's
                     ADJUSTED PRICE RANGE (TRUE High - ACTUAL Low)
                 (2) The TRUE PRICE RANGE (TRUE High - TRUE Low) is
                     GREATER THAN:      5^6
                 (3) The CLOSE is LESS THAN:    232^4
                 (4) AND AT LEAST ONE of these two conditions is TRUE
                 (4A) TODAY's TRUE PRICE RANGE is GREATER THAN:     5^6
                 (4B) TODAY's LOW is LESS THAN:    231^2

W__MAR95--->>>  Current Position: FLAT     Entry Date/Price: ------ -------
         --->>>  NO TRADE SIGNALS AT THIS TIME   <<<---

S__MAR95--->>>  Current Position: FLAT     Entry Date/Price: ------ -------
         --->>>  Sell Signal: Sell Stop at:   569^4  LIMIT:    558^0
         --->>>>>EXIT on DAY of ENTRY [BUY MOC] IF:
                 (1) The CLOSE is within the UPPER ONE FOURTH of the DAY's
                     ACTUAL PRICE RANGE (ACTUAL High - ACTUAL Low)
                 (2) AND AT LEAST ONE of these two conditions is TRUE
                 (2A) The CLOSE is GREATER THAN:   570^0
                 (2B) TODAY's ACTUAL PRICE RANGE is GREATER THAN:    11^6

BO_MAR95--->>>  Current Position: LONG     Entry Date/Price: 941223    27.36
         --->>>  Exit Signal: Sell Stop at:   26.83
         --->>>>>EXIT TODAY on the CLOSE [SELL MOC] IF:
                 (1) The CLOSE is within the LOWER ONE FOURTH of the DAY's
                     ADJUSTED PRICE RANGE (TRUE High - ACTUAL Low)
                 (2) The TRUE PRICE RANGE (TRUE High - TRUE Low) is
                     GREATER THAN:     1.17
                 (3) The CLOSE is LESS THAN:    28.26
                 (4) AND AT LEAST ONE of these two conditions is TRUE
                 (4A) TODAY's TRUE PRICE RANGE is GREATER THAN:     .89
                 (4B) TODAY's LOW is LESS THAN:    27.71

SM_MAR95--->>>  Current Position: FLAT     Entry Date/Price: ------ -------
         --->>>  Sell Signal: Sell Stop at:   161.6  LIMIT:    158.3
         --->>>>>EXIT on DAY of ENTRY [BUY MOC] IF:
                 (1) The CLOSE is within the UPPER ONE FOURTH of the DAY's
                     ACTUAL PRICE RANGE (ACTUAL High - ACTUAL Low)
                 (2) AND AT LEAST ONE of these two conditions is TRUE
                 (2A) The CLOSE is GREATER THAN:    161.8
                 (2B) TODAY's ACTUAL PRICE RANGE is GREATER THAN:    3.1

O__MAR95--->>>  Current Position: FLAT     Entry Date/Price: ------ -------
         --->>>  Sell Signal: Sell Stop at:   122^6  LIMIT:    116^6
         --->>>>>EXIT on DAY of ENTRY [BUY MOC] IF:
                 (1) The CLOSE is within the UPPER ONE FOURTH of the DAY's
                     ACTUAL PRICE RANGE (ACTUAL High - ACTUAL Low)
                 (2) AND AT LEAST ONE of these two conditions is TRUE
                 (2A) The CLOSE is GREATER THAN:    123^2
                 (2B) TODAY's ACTUAL PRICE RANGE is GREATER THAN:    3^4
```

Figure 21–2   Open Trades Report

```
---> P A T T E R N    P R O B A B I L I T Y    S T R A T E G Y   <---

                         Open Trades Report

                   At Close of Trading on 12-27-1994
```

Market	Position	Entry Date	Entry Price	Current Price	Stop Price	P/L	Margin
US_MAR95	LONG	941202	97^30	100^21	99^09	2720	2700
MB_MAR95	LONG	941223	85^04	86^01	85^04	900	2700
ED_MAR95	SHORT	941222	92.91	92.81	92.95	250	675
JY_MAR95	SHORT	941125	102.36	100.49	100.85	2338	1688
CD_MAR95	SHORT	941115	73.56	71.33	72.09	2230	810
GC_FEB95	SHORT	941223	382.1	383.3	384.4	(119)	1330
SI_MAR95	SHORT	941221	482.5	482.5	490.5	0	1064
C_MAR95	LONG	941223	231^4	232^4	229^0	50	540
BO_MAR95	LONG	941223	27.36	28.26	26.83	540	540

```
            <<<<<  Total Open P/L:    8908  >>>>>
            <<<<<  Total Margin:     12047  >>>>>
```

Figure 21–3   Today's Trades Report

```
---> P A T T E R N    P R O B A B I L I T Y    S T R A T E G Y   <---

                        Today's Trades Report

                  Trades Entered/Exited on 12-27-1994
```

Market	Trade	Entry Date	Entry Price	Current or Exit	Stop Price	P/L	Margin
HU_MAR95	EXIT S	941215	51.45	52.20	–	(315)	1500

Figure 21–4   New Signals Report

```
---> P A T T E R N    P R O B A B I L I T Y    S T R A T E G Y   <---

                        New Signals Report

          Signals generated 12-27-1994 for trading on 12-28-1994

       NOTE --- Consult the DAILY SIGNALS Report for STOPs and LIMITs
```

Market	Signal Position	Entry Price	Current Price
HG_MAR95	BUY	136.00	135.45
S_MAR95	SELL	569^4	576^6
SM_MAR95	SELL	161.6	161.9
O_MAR95	SELL	122^6	127^4
CL_MAR95	SELL	16.87	17.60
HU_MAR95	SELL	50.85	52.95
HO_MAR95	SELL	48.70	49.85

Figure 21–5   Performance Summary Report

```
---> P A T T E R N    P R O B A B I L I T Y    S T R A T E G Y   <---
                      Performance Summary Report
                 --->   US_JAN99 <> OPT-0001   <---

                                 LONG'S      SHORT'S     SUMMARY
                                 ------      -------     -------

         NUMBER OF TRADES:          23          19          42
         NUMBER OF PROFITABLE TRADES:  13        8          21
         PERCENT PROFITABLE TRADES:  56.5%     42.1%       50.0%
         TOTAL PROFIT:            18,813      11,281      30,094
         TOTAL LOSS:             -4,063      -4,250      -8,313
         LARGEST PROFIT:          5,250       8,281       8,281
         LARGEST LOSS:             -875        -594        -875
         MAXIMUM DRAWDOWN:       -2,000      -2,063      -2,000
         AVERAGE PROFIT PER TRADE:   641        370         519
         AVERAGE PROFIT/LOSS RATIO:  3.56       3.65        3.62
         TOTAL NET PROFIT:       14,750       7,031      21,781
         PERFORMANCE FACTOR:     ------      ------        2.25

          [ START DATE: 891101 <<--->> END DATE: 940901 ]
```

```
Entry.VarA:                   34.00
Entry.VarC:                   20.00
Entry.VarD:                   10.00
Entry.VarE:                   38.00
Entry.VarF:                    2.00
Entry.VarG:                   10.00
Entry.VarH:                    1.00
Entry.VarJ:                   28.00

ReNtry.VarA:                  10.00
ReNtry.VarB:                   6.00

ExitBreakEvenRange.VarA:      98.00
ExitBreakEvenRange.VarC:      20.00

ExitBigCTReversal.VarA:       25.00

SetUpDayCounter1.VarA:        40.00

FlagPoleCounter2.VarA:        20.00

MaxRiskDollarValue:            400
BreakEvenTargetDollarValue:    800
```

Figure 21-6   Historical Trade Listing

```
      ---> P A T T E R N   P R O B A B I L I T Y   S T R A T E G Y   <---

                       Historical Trade Listing

                    ---> US_JAN99 <> OPT-0001 <---
```

Date	Action	Current Price	Trade P/L	Net Profit	Maximum Drawdown	Trade Code
891101,	BUY,	83^10,	,	,	,	11
891103,	EXIT,	82^30,	-375,	-375,	-375,	25
891108,	BUY,	83^17,	,	,	,	11
891109,	EXIT,	83^05,	-375,	-750,	-750,	25
891115,	BUY,	83^24,	,	,	,	11
891116,	EXIT,	83^12,	-375,	-1125,	-1125,	25
900309,	SELL,	75^19,	,	,	,	11
900314,	EXIT,	75^19,	0,	-1125,	-1125,	25
900613,	BUY,	77^31,	,	,	,	11
900615,	EXIT,	77^31,	0,	-1125,	-1125,	25
900723,	SELL,	76^31,	,	,	,	11
900726,	EXIT,	77^11,	-375,	-1500,	-1500,	25
900806,	SELL,	76^12,	,	,	,	12
900907,	EXIT,	73^20,	2750,	1250,	-1500,	24
900911,	SELL,	72^31,	,	,	,	11
900912,	EXIT,	73^18,	-594,	656,	-1500,	25
900913,	SELL,	73^07,	,	,	,	11
900928,	EXIT,	73^02,	156,	813,	-1500,	24
901029,	BUY,	75^24,	,	,	,	11
901029,	EXIT,	74^28,	-875,	-63,	-1500,	20
901101,	BUY,	76^03,	,	,	,	11
901107,	EXIT,	76^03,	0,	-63,	-1500,	25
901112,	BUY,	77^09,	,	,	,	12
901220,	EXIT,	80^16,	3219,	3156,	-1500,	24
910429,	BUY,	81^13,	,	,	,	11
910429,	EXIT,	81^07,	-188,	2969,	-1500,	20
910621,	SELL,	78^23,	,	,	,	11
910628,	EXIT,	79^03,	-375,	2594,	-1500,	25
910705,	SELL,	78^29,	,	,	,	11
910711,	EXIT,	79^09,	-375,	2219,	-1500,	25
910906,	BUY,	84^04,	,	,	,	11
911009,	EXIT,	86^09,	2156,	4375,	-1500,	24
911219,	BUY,	89^02,	,	,	,	11
920114,	EXIT,	91^04,	2063,	6438,	-1500,	24
920211,	SELL,	88^20,	,	,	,	11
920227,	EXIT,	88^19,	31,	6469,	-1500,	22
920722,	BUY,	92^22,	,	,	,	11
920824,	EXIT,	95^06,	2500,	8969,	-1500,	24
921105,	SELL,	93^07,	,	,	,	11
921106,	EXIT,	93^19,	-375,	8594,	-1500,	25
921109,	SELL,	92^16,	,	,	,	12
921110,	EXIT,	92^28,	-375,	8219,	-1500,	25
921221,	BUY,	96^24,	,	,	,	11
921229,	EXIT,	96^24,	0,	8219,	-1500,	25
930104,	BUY,	97^11,	,	,	,	11
930107,	EXIT,	96^31,	-375,	7844,	-1500,	25
930119,	BUY,	97^31,	,	,	,	11
930121,	EXIT,	97^19,	-375,	7469,	-1500,	25
930122,	BUY,	98^16,	,	,	,	12
930312,	EXIT,	103^24,	5250,	12719,	-1500,	24
930323,	BUY,	104^13,	,	,	,	11

Figure 21–6   **Historical Trade Listing (continued)**

930324,	EXIT,	104^01,	−375,	12344,	−1500,	25
930809,	BUY,	110^23,	,	,	,	11
930813,	EXIT,	110^23,	0,	12344,	−1500,	25
930819,	BUY,	111^12,	,	,	,	11
930820,	EXIT,	111^00,	−375,	11969,	−1500,	25
930823,	BUY,	112^07,	,	,	,	12
930909,	EXIT,	115^18,	3344,	15313,	−1500,	23
930927,	BUY,	114^21,	,	,	,	11
930930,	EXIT,	114^21,	0,	15313,	−1500,	25
931008,	BUY,	115^31,	,	,	,	11
931021,	EXIT,	116^08,	281,	15594,	−1500,	24
931119,	SELL,	111^14,	,	,	,	11
931123,	EXIT,	111^14,	0,	15594,	−1500,	25
940103,	SELL,	111^19,	,	,	,	11
940105,	EXIT,	111^24,	−156,	15438,	−1500,	25
940127,	BUY,	113^22,	,	,	,	11
940201,	EXIT,	113^22,	0,	15438,	−1500,	25
940217,	SELL,	111^23,	,	,	,	11
940406,	EXIT,	103^14,	8281,	23719,	−1500,	23
940506,	SELL,	101^31,	,	,	,	11
940516,	EXIT,	101^29,	63,	23781,	−1500,	22
940527,	SELL,	101^28,	,	,	,	11
940531,	EXIT,	102^12,	−500,	23281,	−1500,	25
940617,	SELL,	102^05,	,	,	,	11
940620,	EXIT,	102^17,	−375,	22906,	−1500,	25
940624,	SELL,	101^14,	,	,	,	11
940627,	EXIT,	101^26,	−375,	22531,	−1500,	25
940630,	SELL,	101^04,	,	,	,	11
940707,	EXIT,	101^04,	0,	22531,	−1500,	25
940711,	SELL,	99^13,	,	,	,	12
940712,	EXIT,	99^25,	−375,	22156,	−1625,	25
940831,	BUY,	102^31,	,	,	,	11
940901,	EXIT,	102^19,	−375,	21781,	−2000,	25

When performing historical testing, you may wish to try several sets of parameter settings so you can later compare performance based upon different settings. That option is available in the PPS program. The program will display a list of the tested parameter sets, ranked according to performance in each of three different performance categories. Using this method of multiple-loop selections, one can create a unique and individualized trading system.

Performance reports list net profit, average profit per trade, and performance factor. Net profit is the sum of all winning trades minus all losing trades. Average profit is the net profit divided by the total number of trades. Performance factor is the annualized net profit divided by the maximum drawdown.

Customizing PPS

There are 17 parameter variables in PPS that may be customized by the user. Although these variables are factory set at default settings, there are many reasons one might wish to alter them: 1) Some of the variables act as filters; by changing settings one can limit the number of trades that the system generates and become more conservative or let more trades through in order to trade more aggressively; 2) A trader may wish to specialize in a particular commodity complex. As commodity complexes and individual markets exhibit individual trading personalities, it would not be unexpected that superior settings could be found; 3) A trader may wish to ensure that his own PPS system is unique. Given that the possible permutations of variables and settings are in the millions, the user can create his own masterpiece.

To give you a feel for how you could approach the customization process, I will briefly discuss each of the variables.

Variable #1: Maximum Slope Allowance—This filter determines how "steep" the trend-line slope is allowed to be. Larger numbers allow steeper slopes; smaller numbers require the slope to be flatter. If, for example, one only wanted to buy ascending triangle formations, he could set the value to about 5; only patterns with nearly flat upper trend lines would generate signals. Conversely, for sells, only descending triangles with nearly flat lower trend lines would generate signals.

Variable #2: Reverse Slope Allowance—Similar to Variable #1, this variable allows a certain "reverse" slope. This is for situations where, for example, a buy pattern's upper trend line is beyond flat and actually slopes upwards. By setting the variable to zero, the user eliminates reverse slope trend line signals.

Variable #3: Multiple of Range for Signal Protective Stop—In addition to a monetary stop loss (Variable #16), the software also employs a stop that is a multiple of the universal average range. While the money management stop is the overriding stop, this stop is unique in that it works in harmony with the volatility of each particular market.

Variable #4: Maximum Number of Price Periods—This variable sets the maximum number of bars allowed in any given price pattern. For example, if the user wished to test patterns of 10 days or less, he would set this variable to 10.

Variable #5: Number of Contract Points Plus or Minus Trend Line for Entry Stop—Once a "setup" has occurred, this number will determine how far above (for a buy) or below (for a sell) the trend line to place the entry stop. Small numbers will cause earlier entries; larger numbers require more confirmation of the trend line break before a position is initiated.

Variable #6: Counter Number after Which No Reset—If we have a pattern in formation and we get another signal to begin a new pattern, do we abandon the present one for a new one, or do we ignore the new potential pattern? By controlling this number, the user can control the answer to that question.

Variable #7: Checking Loop—Technical purists may only want to take signals that are generated from "unbroken" trend lines. This variable is a switch that is either on or off. When on, this function looks to see if the entry trend line has been drawn through other bars. If it has, no signal is generated. The off position draws trend-lines from point 1 to point 2, regardless of how many bars may be sticking through it.

Variable #8: Trend Filter Average—Number of Days—A simple moving average of closes. The requirement for a buy is that the entry point be above this average; for a sell, the entry point must be below it.

Variable #9: Maximum Number of Price Periods Since Prior Trade Entry for Reentry—This is one of the variables that controls the reentry signal. Sometimes after an entry, the trade will be stopped out, only to see the market reverse and go to new highs (for a buy) or new lows (for a sell) without otherwise generating a signal from a trend line break. This variable limits the number of bars since the previous trade's entry in which this reentry is allowed.

Variable #10: Maximum Number of Price Periods Since Prior Trade Exit for Reentry—This variable is similar to Variable #9, the difference being that this variable only limits the number of bars since the previous trade's *exit* in which to allow a reentry.

Variable #11: Exit Break-Even Range—Percent of Profit Willing to Risk—Once the price range triggers a break-even exit stop placement, this variable selects how much of the maximum trade profit to risk. When the variable is set to 100, 100 percent of the profit is at risk (true breakeven). A setting of 50 would cause the trade to be exited if one-half of the maximum profit was lost, and so on.

Variable #12: Multiple of Average Range Where Break-Even Range Protective Stop Begins—This variable determines after what multiple of average range the break-even stop becomes active.

Variable #13: Multiple of Average Range Today's Range Must Be for Exit—This variable determines the minimum multiple of average range for one particular exit to come into effect. This exit calls for exiting the market at the close if a wide-range day has occurred that closes near the low (for longs). The default of 25 requires the reversal-day's range to be 2.5 times the average. Smaller numbers will generate more reversal exits; a large number, like 60, will virtually eliminate this exit.

Variable #14: Global Average Range—Number of Days—This is a critical variable: Its setting determines the number of days to use in the average true-range calculation. Determinations such as whether and where to enter or exit a position are made based on this variable.

Variable #15: Amount of #1 Point Break Allowed before Reset—The signal to reset the counter on a particular pattern, other than when maximum number of price periods is exceeded (Variable #4), is when the highest high of the pattern is broken (for a buy). Variable #15 allows a break without reset by a certain fraction of the average range, allowing for small "false breaks." A setting of 20 equals two-tenths of the average range, 50 equals one-half the average range, and a setting of zero would reset the counter when there is *any* break of the highest high.

Variable #16: Money Management Stop—This variable determines the maximum dollar amount to risk per trade and overrides all other stops. It is one of the more frequently adjusted variables by users.

Variable #17: Break-Even Stop—This variable sets the dollar amount which, once achieved (intraday), brings the protective stop to at least breakeven, based on computer entry price.

Chapter 22

The Nature and Purpose of Diversification

> *The behavior of commodity markets has changed greatly in the 1990s due to the globalization of markets. As a result, diversification must be looked at in a new light.*

The Universe of Futures Markets

In Chapter 9, Fast-Start Portfolio, I listed 36 different markets and briefly commented on their applicability to the PPS approach. Are there still more markets to trade? *Yes*. There are literally hundreds of futures markets on dozens of exchanges throughout the world, and more contracts are being designed every day. Indeed, a large number of PPS traders are foreign-based and do extremely well trading the bond contracts of Germany, France, England, Italy, Australia, and Japan. Most major stock markets have an associated futures contract as well.

In the first 10-year computerized historical test of PPS (1979 to 1989), we selected a portfolio of 18 markets; those were about all that were liquid and on-line for the entire period. Our results showed that, over that period, every one of the 18 markets was profitable.

In real-time trading, I began expanding the portfolio as new market contracts emerged or gained liquidity. Natural gas is one example of a futures market that did not exist during the earlier historical test, but came into its own shortly thereafter. Eventually, my portfolio expanded to 30 markets. I rationalized that, by trading more markets, I would have more opportunities to get on board a trend. Of course, I knew better than to trade highly correlated markets at the same time. For example, if I had signals in the D-mark, Swiss Franc, and Dollar Index at the same time, I would only take one; the same would hold true if signals occurred in crude, heating oil, and unleaded gas, or if signals occurred in soybeans, soybean meal, and bean oil.

I would typically handle the "multiple signal" situation by taking the signal in the strongest market (for longs) and weakest market (for shorts). I coached students to do the same. But sometimes it was difficult to determine which market was the strongest or weakest. Over what time frame—the last three days? the last two weeks? the last month? Certainly, I had applied subjective filtering. If others had as well, trading results among individual PPS traders could vary dramatically.

The fact that each individual's experience with PPS could be different did not concern me. After all, I had always presented PPS as a methodology, and I felt that the flexibility it offered was a plus. What did concern me struck much closer to home. As I began to trade an increasing number of markets, I would sometimes find myself holding positions in as many as 10 to 12 markets. Then, on any given day, all my positions would go against me.

These severe one-day drawdowns were extremely unsettling. Eventually, the positions would work themselves out: Most would be stopped out, but a few would go on to make big money. After a while, I would forget about that "bad day." But then, before too long, it would happen again. I must be a slow learner; this went on for well over a year before it dawned on me that something was wrong. Something was different about the markets. After all, it just didn't make any sense that all those unrelated markets could change their fundamentals at the same time. Why was this occurring?

The Globalization Factor

The world is changing, and so are financial markets. In futures markets, even the players are changing, and the players are who make markets. What I had been learning—the hard way—was that there is a trend toward increasing correlation among markets which, based on their individual fundamentals, should *not* be correlated.

In years past, one could trade individual markets based entirely on their particular fundamentals and technicals. There were more small traders and individual traders. Now, however, behemoth global interests have entered the futures markets to such an extent that open interest limits have recently been expanded in many markets to accommodate them. In years past, trends would develop slowly, as individual traders would become ever more bullish or bearish on a particular market because of developing fundamentals. Now, with instant communication and very large trading interests, bullish or bearish sentiment can sweep through the entire commodity complex in minutes—regardless of the fundamentals present in the individual markets. Why does this take place?

The first significant correlation between markets occurred quite a few years ago, when traders started to notice that their individual market was reacting not just to its own fundamentals and technicals, but also to the bond market. So after awhile, regardless of what market was traded, one had to also watch the bond market.

Then, when stock indexes became popular, traders saw correlations occur between the bond market and stock indexes, so one had to keep an eye on the S&P 500 futures contract as well.

Sometimes, though, there seemed to be no correlation, and that was often because of movement in the dollar. Now, it became important to watch the bonds, S&P, and dollar contracts—because regardless of what market one was trading, the position could be affected by sudden movements in *any* of those markets.

Of course, now German and Japanese markets affect our own. And global energy prices affect all markets. Attempting to figure out the thousands of possible correlations is simply *not possible*. One must accept the fact that bizarre price movements—not based on an individual market's fundamentals or technicals—can and do occur with increasing regularity.

New Computer Research

By early 1994, our in-house computer research facility had developed programs that allowed us to analyze the PPS System in new ways. One program allowed us to test all markets using PPS and rank them from best to worst over any historical test period. Another program allowed us to construct a portfolio of any size and composition and obtain an equity curve for that portfolio. The more we examined the results of our tests, the more it became clear that my "more is better" supposition was not correct. The computer was telling us that, depending upon the markets selected, the optimum portfolio might lie in the five- to nine-market range. A portfolio in excess of that, given the increase in correlation we've seen in recent years, would be highly redundant and would not increase overall profitability.

There are several advantages to a smaller portfolio: 1) Diversification is still preserved; 2) Because fewer trades are open at one time, a larger percentage of capital may be allocated to each trade; 3) Fewer trades means lower total commissions and slippage; 4) Concentration in only the larger, more liquid markets reduces slippage; and 5) Drawdowns may be reduced during periods of general market choppiness.

The new programs appeared to be a way to help us devise an optimum portfolio based on predetermined input criteria. If so, PPS would not only offer a greater degree of customization and flexibility, but these new tools would allow the user to quickly reassess his portfolio assumptions as changing conditions dictated.

Chapter 23

Creating a Winning Portfolio

The PPS Portfolio Analyzer was created in 1994. For the first time, we could graphically depict PPS trading results of any market or any portfolio. What lessons did we learn about market selection and portfolio construction?

Just as it can be said that no one system is right for everybody, it can also be said, even among PPS traders, that no one *portfolio* is right for everybody. Numerous factors can influence one's decisions while creating a portfolio.

One should have some kind of macroeconomic perspective upon which to base his selection process, rather that simply finding market combinations that worked in the past. An example of a macroeconomic perspective would be someone who expected real estate prices to remain flat into the future. That person would not be served by buying real estate, even if his investments were diversified geographically or by type.

So an investor who comes to the futures market may have some fundamental viewpoints that will influence his portfolio selection. A "gold bug" may construct a portfolio heavily weighted in the precious metals or even restrict his signals to only long trades in that complex; a grain farmer could have strong opinions about that particular group of markets in which he is an expert.

A second factor that is crucial in constructing a portfolio is the size of the account. A small account will require fewer markets in the portfolio. Otherwise, the potential drawdown could be too severe and a margin call could result. The trader needs to be able to judge, based on historical precedent, what size drawdown he will likely encounter.

The trader must also decide if he intends to trade aggressively or conservatively. An honest assessment will help the trader construct a portfolio that is right for him. It will do the trader no good to pack his portfolio with high-octane markets if he cannot psychologically withstand the corresponding drawdowns that may be associated with that portfolio.

PPS Portfolio Analyzer

Fortunately, by late 1994, we were able to take our internal research programs and combine them into a user-friendly, Windows-based program available for commercial use; the program was called the PPS Portfolio Analyzer.

Once I saw it run the first time, I didn't know how we had ever lived without it. Prior to the Portfolio Analyzer, historical testing with the original PPS Software would allow the user to test markets only individually, not in portfolios. Therefore, although PPS had always been praised for its low drawdowns, we had no way to access what those drawdowns actually were for given portfolios. Now, suddenly, graphs and reports were available that provided enough information to make intelligent portfolio choices.

It soon became clear that I had literally been wasting my time trading grain markets and precious metals. Overall, the price of grain has been declining for almost 20 years, due to overproduction. Occasionally, weather markets will cause some excitement, but it is usually short-lived. Among most grain markets, the recent decade (1984–1994) saw only one major bull market, and that was in 1988. Precious metals began a major bear market in 1980 and have been under siege since inflation fears subsided and a recession mentality took hold in the late 1980s. If you remember, PPS makes nearly twice as much money in bull markets than in bear markets. In general, then, unless a market is starting from a very high level, bear markets are nothing to get excited about in commodities.

As early as 1993, I began to hear reports from PPS traders around the world who were making big money trading their own foreign markets, typically their bonds, stock indices, and world currency markets. Meanwhile, PPS traders in the United States were trading about 30 markets—and many were going nowhere. What's more, if I'd had the PPS Portfolio Analyzer sooner, I might have realized that some of the markets we were trading had contributed very little to the bottom line in years. In hindsight, a more up-to-date portfolio would have made both myself and my U.S.-based students even more money.

The fact is that during the last decade, the financial markets—currencies and interest rates—have offered the best opportunities for PPS traders, and trend followers in general. A reasonable amount of money has been made in the petroleum complex, and diverse markets such as coffee, orange juice, and lumber have each shown a proclivity for spectacular trends, both up and down.

But what about the future? My expectations are that we will see these same markets continue to offer profitable trends; Figure 23–1 illustrates why. You will note that the portfolio selected is fairly well diversified: three currency contracts, two petroleum contracts, two interest rate contracts, two food contracts, and one fiber contract. The chart assumes we started with a $25,000 account and that we traded only one contract throughout the 10-year test. After deducting $75 for slippage and commission, the net profit was $307,676. That equates to an average return of 123 percent per year.

Running the same portfolio over just the last five years, the total profit was $136,612. That equates to an average return of 109 percent per year. The degradation from one five-year period to the next is minimal. That becomes even more evident when you examine additional statistics: The winning percentage was 29.76 during the 10-year test and 28.90 during the most recent five years. The average win/loss ratio was 5.46 during the 10-year test and 4.98 during the most recent five years. This strongly suggests that not only the PPS system but this particular portfolio is extremely robust.

Staying Current

Relying solely on the past can eventually become a recipe for disaster. I repeat: The truly successful trader will be the one who formulates his own macroeconomic framework for the future and is correct in his prognostication.

Figure 23–1   **Diversified 10-Market Portfolio,**
                    10-Year Test, Single Contracts

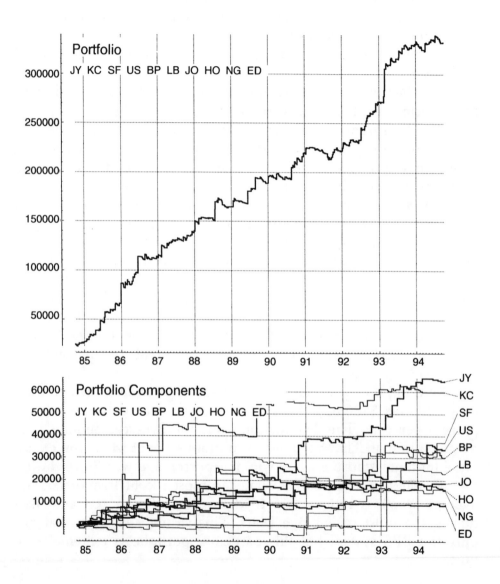

That is not to say that a system trader cannot make a great deal of money over a period of time using what has been presented in this book. But the wise trader will keep an ear to the ground and be ready to adjust his portfolio as geopolitical occurrences dictate. One day, inflation might return with a vengeance, and the metals markets will become active and profitable for trend traders. Or weather patterns could become so disturbed as to cause severe crop damage for several years running, thus depleting the swollen inventories that have become commonplace. An unexpected war could also ignite otherwise dormant markets. The astute trader must never become complacent about his portfolio.

Fortunately, by using the PPS Portfolio Analyzer, the trader can recognize when a particular market is not contributing its share toward the overall profitability of the portfolio. By testing different markets, he may see other markets, currently not in his portfolio, that may be better candidates.

Common Sense

Creating a winning portfolio does not simply mean taking the top-performing markets and using those in your portfolio; diversification is still very important. Had I created a portfolio of only currencies, I'm sure that the results would have been quite remarkable—but would I have a diversified portfolio? The Swiss Franc and the D-mark, two highly correlated markets, would essentially duplicate each other. And sometimes all the foreign currencies run in a pack against the U.S. dollar. Without diversification, the portfolio could be subjected to nightmarish drawdowns. Fortunately, the PPS Portfolio Analyzer allows the trader to create any portfolio and then examine the drawdown both in actual dollar as well as percentage terms. This is critical when deciding how much capitalization will be required.

Long or Short?

Another feature of the PPS Portfolio Analyzer is that for any individual market, the trader cannot only take all the trades generated by the PPS Trading System, but can test the effect of taking only long trades or only short trades. This feature allows the trader to exercise his own creativity.

What if you decided you wanted to have gold in your portfolio but that you only wanted to take the long trades? Or you could go one step further: By examining the trade-by-trade detailed report summary, you could eliminate short trades below a certain price level—for example, $400 in gold, $6 in soybeans, $5 in silver, and so on. In the same way, a seasonally oriented trader could eliminate trades—either long or short—during certain seasons. Thus this tool allows the trader to incorporate *fundamental viewpoints into his technical* trading system.

Summary

The PPS Portfolio Analyzer has truly given each PPS trader the ability to create a unique portfolio that incorporates 1) his market preferences, 2) his need for diversification, 3) his personal aversion to risk, 4) his capitalization, and 5) his unique fundamental views. What an exciting prospect for any trader!

But the excitement is just beginning—I've saved the very best for last. Back in Chapter 3, I talked about what you must do to acquire commodity wealth. I said that *you must think long-term*, and that *you must utilize the power of compounding*.

You may want to refresh your memory by turning back to review the Power of Compounding table. When this concept is firmly planted in your mind, you will be ready to go on to the final chapter—the chapter that will clearly demonstrate the power of the PPS Trading System to literally create a fortune in a relatively short period of time.

C h a p t e r   2 4

Fixed-Fractional Trading

> *The fixed-fractional approach is a powerful money management technique which, when combined with PPS, has been shown to generate exponential equity curves.*

Definition

Fixed-fractional trading means that you risk the same percentage of your capital on each trade. For example, assume you have a $25,000 account and you are trading single contracts. There is a buy signal in corn at $5.50, based on a symmetrical triangle. You draw in the apex line and determine that your stop should be at $4.47. Because the value of the contract is $50 per cent, your total risk would be $150 plus commission.

Taking the same example, assume that you are trading fixed fractionally, and have decided to risk 2 percent of your capital on each trade. Based on a $25,000 account, you will risk $500 on each trade. In the corn trade, you would trade three contracts ($500/$150 = 3.33 contracts). What if the stop were at $4.45? In that case, you would trade two contracts ($500/$250 = 2.0 contracts).

Benefits

Benefit #1: **The fixed-fractional approach equally weights risk among all your positions.** Without a fixed-fractional approach, the risk in your portfolio will generally be weighted toward those markets with higher margin requirements. For example, a corn trade (one contract) may be underweighted relative to a D-mark trade (one contract). Such weighting discrepancies can work in your favor or against you, depending upon what markets show good or bad performance in any given year.

In recent years, the unintentional weighting of the single contract approach may have actually benefited PPS traders because currencies (higher margin contracts) outperformed grains (lower margin contracts). But there are many other markets to consider—all with differing margins. In the 10-market portfolio we examined in the last chapter, one of the contracts was Eurodollars. To equally weight a Eurodollar position and a T-bond position, more Eurodollar contracts would be required, due to their lower margin. The fixed-fractional approach makes this adjustment automatically.

Benefit #2: **The fixed-fractional approach is more efficient.** Assume, again, that you begin trading single contracts with a $25,000 account. You do well, and your account grows to $40,000. When do you start trading two contracts? A simple answer might be when you get to $50,000. But if that is the case, when you are trading one contract with $40,000, you are *under*trading relative to your capital. Give this some thought. If, indeed, you intend to wait until you have $50,000 before you trade two contracts, then what happens when your account is at $49,000? Would it make sense to trade one contract with $49,000 and then risk twice as much when your account is $1,000 higher? The fixed-fractional approach eliminates such dilemmas.

Benefit #3: **The fixed-fractional approach automatically adjusts your risk/reward to market volatility.** When market volatility is low, patterns are more compact, and the initial stop can be closer to the entry. This is, however, of little advantage to the single-contract trader. Remember our corn illustration: Despite only a $150 risk, the single-contract trader was limited to one contract, while the fixed-fractional trader was able to trade three contracts. This is in keeping with PPS theory, which states that we should attempt to board trends when volatility is low and risk is less.

On the other hand, if the market has become volatile and a pattern forms, the stop is likely to be further away than when the market was less volatile. The single-contract trader and the fixed-fractional trader may then each trade one contract, the fixed-fractional trader having *decreased* the number of contracts in accordance with volatility.

Benefit #4: **Combining the fixed-fractional approach with PPS, it is almost impossible not to achieve success over the long term.** Futures trading is a highly leveraged activity. The typical beginning trader is so overconfident that he overlooks the fact that leverage is a two-edged sword: He thinks about how much money he will make, rather than how much he could lose. It is almost comical that the beginning trader, despite knowing full well that 90 percent of all traders lose money, fully believes that *he* will be among the 10 percent who make money.

That overconfidence often causes him to risk too much relative to his account size. Before he knows it, a sizable percentage of his account has been lost. Often he does not fully appreciate the most important money management concept: *The percent gain needed to recover a loss increases geometrically with the loss.* For example, if you lose 15 percent of your capital, a gain of 17.6 percent on your remaining capital is then required in order to get even. If you lose 30 percent, a gain of 42.9 percent will be required; and, if you lose 50 percent, a gain of 100 percent is required (see Table 24–1).

The beauty of the fixed-fractional approach is that when your trading is not going well, the dollar amount that you risk *decreases* in direct proportion to the size of your trading account. In theory, this makes it very difficult to go broke. For example, if you started with $100,000 and risked 2 percent per trade, you would risk $2,000 per trade initially. But, if the account decreased to $60,000, you would still risk 2 percent—which would then be only $1,200 per trade. By cutting back your risk when the value of your account declines, you will be able to stay in the game longer.

If your $100,000 account, instead, increased in value—say, to $140,000—the fixed-fractional approach would increase your risk to $2,800 per trade. Accordingly, you would now be trading a larger number of contracts. If you hit a run of profitable trades, your profits would rapidly compound upon themselves.

It is quite possible, however, that when you do encounter a string of losses, your drawdown will be more severe. This occurs because, when you do hit a losing streak, you are trading a maximum number of contracts. The excessive drawdown potential may, at first, seem like a contradiction; didn't we say that one of the advantages of the fixed-fractional approach was that it made it diffi-

Table 24–1   **Recovery Table**

Percent of Loss of Initial Capital	Percent Gain on Balance Required to Recover Loss
5	5.3
10	11.1
15	17.6
20	25.0
25	33.3
30	42.9
35	53.8
40	66.7
45	81.8
50	100.0
55	122.0
60	150.0
65	186.0
70	233.0
75	300.0
80	400.0
85	567.0
90	900.0

cult to go broke? Absolutely. But going broke and having a severe drawdown are quite different. By definition, a severe drawdown is only possible after a positive run in which your account reaches a higher plateau. If your account were to decline from its *initial* value, the decline would be *less* severe than a single contract approach.

Practical Applications

Before going further, please examine Figure 24–1, which shows our 10-market portfolio, tested this time over only the last five

Figure 24–1   **Diversified Ten Market Portfolio, Five-Year Test, 2 Percent Fixed Fractional**

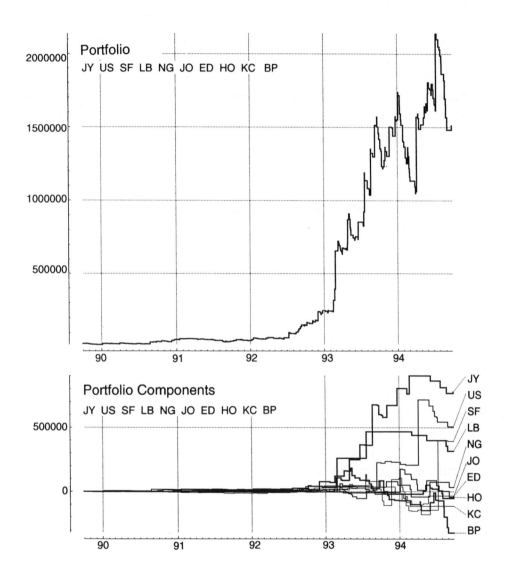

years—but with one difference being the use of a fixed-fractional 2 percent risk per trade. This is the same time period that produced a total profit of $136,612 trading single contracts.

Surprised? No, those numbers are not a misprint. In only five years, and with a risk of only 2 percent of capital for each trade, PPS took a $25,000 account to $1,487,184. Actually, the account exceeded two million dollars before succumbing to a drawdown in the third quarter of 1994. Could you have done it? Let's find out.

Looking again at the graph, you'll notice that the curve looks relatively flat for the first three years and then explodes in 1993. This phenomenon has practically nothing to do with market conditions; the exponential growth is a function of the *compounding!* You can prove this to yourself by examining the same five-year time frame in Table 24–1. Still not convinced? Go back to the compounding table, Table 3–1. If you were to graph the column under 50 percent, you would get the same type of exponential curve, despite the fact that the growth rate each year was a constant 50 percent.

Intellectually, you must concede that it is certainly possible to make two million dollars in five years starting with only $25,000. And Larry Williams is living proof that a *human* can do it. This legendary trader actually took a $10,000 account to over two million dollars in *one* year. But could *you* do it?

Sure, it's possible. But would you really want to live through a $685,831 drawdown? Because that's what it would have taken. And even Larry Williams dropped about $900,000 before finishing the year with a meager million dollars plus in profits. Larry is the kind of guy who can do that, but you're probably not.

So what is the solution? *Have a goal* and *know your limits.* Plan for success and know in advance what you will do when your account reaches a certain level. What do you want out of trading? Is it just a game or is the money important? If the money is important, how much do you hope to make before you cash in your chips? What will you do with the money? You have to answer those questions for yourself. Otherwise, how will you know when you have *won*?

It would be extremely rare to find a trader who has planned for his success well in advance; just as adversity affects a trader psychologically, so does success. Here's how it might affect you. Let's assume you begin trading with $20,000. You decide that if you lose $10,000, you will quit. Why? Maybe because $10,000 means something to you. Maybe losing less is not going to affect your lifestyle, but if you were to lose more, some part of your life might suffer.

What if you are successful, and in a few years your account is up to $200,000? Now, you need to decide if you're willing to risk giving back $100,000—because that could happen. And $100,000 may be significant to you. What do you do? I'll show you. Here's exactly how I made a lot of money using the fixed-fractional approach with PPS—and kept it.

Initially, when my account was small, I risked approximately 2 percent on every trade. As my account grew, I cut back—first going to 1 percent, and finally to ½ of 1 percent. My account continued to grow but at a slower pace. More importantly, I was at peace, knowing that the bulk of my profits were secure due to my very limited risk. You may want to plan a similar strategy.

While this book has progressed in a *theorem and proof* fashion, the focus of this chapter has turned to *money*—real dollars. You probably noticed your heart start to pound a little faster. I can only assume that you are anxious to apply what you have learned. But before you do, take a moment to review your *journey* by reading the following brief summary.

Chapter 25

A Summary of the PPS Trading System

We have now come full circle. Depending on your degree of experience, you may have been challenged by the depth of this presentation. While this would not be considered a beginner's book, I have attempted to make the material as accessible as possible. It might be helpful to review the major ideas set forth, by imagining that you have been on a journey; the journey took you to five different towns, and in each town you gained insights. The insights in each town will have seemed more or less valuable to you, depending upon your prior experience.

In the first town, you discovered how PPS came into being. Then you were exposed to common mistakes that lead the majority of traders to failure. The main insight was that *the one proven way to acquire commodity wealth is to consistently apply a systematic approach and to take advantage of the power of compounding over time.*

In the second town, you learned the basic principles of the PPS approach. You learned a simple way to define the trend, several different entry patterns, and the PPS exit system. After that, you applied what you had learned to actual charts. The main insight was that *by employing certain classical chart patterns and trading with the trend, you can catch major moves while keeping your risks minimal.*

In the third town, you became an expert on classical chart patterns. You learned that much of the conventional wisdom is wrong; you learned what works and what doesn't. You discovered additional patterns that could expand your array of PPS entry signals. The main insight was that *some patterns are much more reliable than others, and by combining several of the highest probability patterns, the PPS entry system would catch most major trends.*

In the fourth town, you learned how to augment the basic mechanical PPS system with a knowledge of commitment of traders data, an awareness of the implications of first notice day and options expiration day, and an understanding of basis and spread relationships. The two main insights were that *1) by applying certain additional technical considerations, the PPS trader can boost his performance to an even higher level, and 2) the psychological demands on the system trader are great, and without a mastery of personal trading discipline, all the knowledge learned will be of little value.*

In the fifth town, the computer was introduced for the first time. Heretofore, while a skeptic could view the PPS principles simply as *theory*, objective computer runs *proved* the profitability and power of PPS beyond a shadow of a doubt. You learned that diversification and portfolio selection will always be key elements that will govern the degree of your success. Finally, you learned how to apply a fixed-fractional money management approach, which would both limit your possibility of failure and boost your compounded returns. The main insight was that *PPS is truly a universal system that each individual trader can customize based on his account size, aggressiveness, and market preferences.*

Whether or not you decide to apply the PPS approach to your trading, I hope that some of the unique research I have compiled, as well as some of my experience, will benefit you.

I wish you good luck—and good trading!

Appendix A

Commodity Sector Historical Test Results

Methodology

This test covered a relatively short period of time—one year from April 1987 to March 1988. The purpose of the test was to examine profitability in individual market sectors. Since I had just begun my PPS trading career in January of 1988, I wanted to have as much detailed information on the recent past as possible.

Grand Totals by Sector

Sector	P/L (units)	# of Trades	Gross Profit per Trade
Grains	128	7	18.3
Softs	238	13	18.3
Metals	67	6	11.2
Interest Rates	162	17	9.5
Currencies	214	18	11.9
Stocks	(13)	3	(4.3)
Oil	67	8	8.4

% Winning Trades—49%

Trades per Year—72

Gross Total Profit—863

Average Gross Profit per Trade—12.0 units

Average Net Profit per Trade—10.0 units

Actual Dollar Profits per Markets and Market Sectors

Grains–$2,457

Corn	(200)
Oats	337
Soybeans	(500)
Bean Meal	960
Bean Oil	1,860

Softs–$9,826

Coffee	1,312
OJ	2,580
Sugar	902
Cotton	4,850
Lumber	182

Metals–$4,700

Gold	2,400
Platinum	2,700
Silver	(400)

Interest Rates–$15,450

Euros	3,200
T-Notes	3,250
T-Bonds	9,500
Munis	(500)

Currencies–$17,874

B.P.	1,675
Can$	75
S.F.	1,562
D.M.	312
J.Y.	14,250

Stock Indexes–$(1,500)

MMI	(1,000)
S&P	(500)

Oil–$6,316

H.O.	(672)
Gas	2,688
Crude	4,300

Total Gross Profit—$55,123

Slippage and Commission—$7,100

Total Net Profit—$48,023

Results are based on trading one contract per signal.

Annualized return based on a $25,000 account—192%

Annualized return deducting largest winning trade—135%

Average length of winning trade—27.1 days

Average length of losing trade—5 days

Average length of all trades—15.9 days

Conclusions

The largest profits during that period came from the softs, with the currencies following in second place. It was encouraging that all sectors did well, excluding stock indexes, which, though tested here, were not part of the PPS portfolio. Other tests, over other time periods, mirrored these results: Currencies and softs have generally proven to be the most profitable sectors.

Appendix B

Individual Market Historical Test Results

Methodology

A majority of PPS signals originate from the symmetrical triangle and ascending triangle. The purpose of this 10-year study (1977–1986) was to examine each of these profitable patterns in individual markets. The data, viewed from this perspective, should reveal 1) which pattern was more profitable, and 2) which markets were more profitable. All numbers are presented as units for purposes of comparison.

Symmetrical Triangle

Market	Profit	Loss
Gold	226	
S&P		7
Cocoa	30	
Sugar	42	
Cotton		8
Coffee	266	
Crude	8	
OJ	230	
Lumber		3
T-Notes		106
Corn	131	
Soybeans	72	
Bean Oil	141	
Bean Meal	329	
Wheat	4	
Copper		8
Silver	230	
Platinum	2	
Eurodollars		5
Swiss Franc	89	
Canadian $	87	
British Pound	100	
Totals	2,096	28

Ascending Triangle

Market	Profit	Loss
Gold	49	
S&P		7
Cocoa	37	
Sugar	31	
Cotton	12	
Coffee	10	
Crude	16	
OJ	114	
Lumber		3
T-Notes		6
Corn		5
Soybeans	11	
Bean Oil	113	
Bean Meal		5
Wheat		3
Copper		5
Silver	27	
Platinum		6
Eurodollars		3
Swiss Franc	28	
Canadian $	21	
British Pound	30	
Totals	508	34

Symmetrical Triangles and Ascending Triangles Combined

Market	Profit	Loss
Gold	275	
S&P		14
Cocoa	67	
Sugar	73	
Cotton	4	
Coffee	276	
Crude	24	
OJ	344	
Lumber		6
T-Notes		112
Corn	126	
Soybeans	83	
Bean Oil	254	
Bean Meal	324	
Wheat	1	
Copper		13
Silver	257	
Platinum		4
Eurodollar		8
Swiss Franc	117	
Canadian $	108	
British Pound	130	
Totals	2,581	39

Top Five Markets
O.J.—344
Bean Meal—324
Coffee—276
Gold—275
Silver—257

Bottom Five Markets
Copper—(13)
Canadian $—(11)
Eurodollars—(8)
S&P—(7)
Platinum—(4)

Conclusions

In answer to our first question, it is no surprise that symmetrical triangles were responsible for approximately four times as much profit as ascending triangles—especially when we remember that symmetrical triangles are three times as numerous. In answer to the second question, more recent data would make it obvious that the most profitable and least profitable markets during that period may not correspond to profitability in more recent times. For example, cotton showed little profitability during the 10-year test but was highly profitable in 1988. Copper was also a net loser during this 10-year test but proved to be the biggest winner of the year during real-time trading in 1988. Portfolio decisions should not be based upon this data. Instead, use the PPS Portfolio Analyzer, which will allow you to test data from 1976 to the present.

A p p e n d i x   C

How to Use the PPS Demo Disk

Note: If you need help loading the program or further explanation of its operation, technical assistance is available from 9 a.m.–5 p.m. EST: (407) 747–1554.

Loading the Program

1. Enter your Windows Program Manager.

2. Click on **File**.

3. Click on **Run**.

4. Depending on whether you are installing from your A drive or B drive, type A:\Install or B:\Install in the dialog box.

5. The PPS Demo program will be loaded on your hard drive into a directory entitled PPSDEMO.

6. To start the program, double click on the "PPS Portfolio Analyzer Demo" icon.

Main Menu

The PPS Demo program is very user-friendly, and you should have no trouble moving around the program. If you are in doubt at any time, just click on **HELP**.

The left side of the Main Menu is for setting up your tests—selecting the markets in the portfolio, the money management, and test period. The right side of the Main Menu is for viewing your results.

WALK-THROUGH TUTORIAL

Setup Analysis

1. Click on **SELECT MARKETS**.

    You will see that the left side of the screen shows which markets have been selected, and the right side shows which markets are available. Because this is a demonstration disk with limited storage capacity, this list is limited to 10 commodities. Their symbols are: British Pound (BP), IMM Eurodollars (ED), Heating Oil (HO), Orange Juice (OJ), Japanese Yen (JY), Coffee (KC), Lumber (LB), Natural Gas (NG), Swiss Franc (SF), and T-Bonds (US). You can select or deselect by pointing to a market, clicking once to highlight it, then clicking on the **add** or **remove** button. To add or remove a consecutive list of markets from the selected or available list, highlight the markets by clicking on a single market with the mouse, then dragging the mouse until the desired group of markets is highlighted. Right now, let's accept the 10 markets already selected by clicking **DONE.**

2. Click on **CHANGE MONEY MANAGEMENT PARAMETERS**.

    The first item, Starting Equity, is currently set to $25,000. If you want to change the account size, point to this item and click once to change the value. The second item, Trade Single Contracts, is set as Yes. This means that, throughout the historical test, the program will assume that only one contract is traded per signal. For now, accept that default by clicking on **OK.**

3. Click on **SET TEST PERIOD START AND STOP DATES**.

    In future tests, you will select your test period by simply pointing to the value, clicking, and typing in any dates you wish. For now, accept the default dates by clicking on **OK.**

View Analysis Results

1. Click on **CREATE EQUITY CURVE**.

    This may take a minute or so, depending on the speed of your computer. An hourglass visible on your screen tells you that processing is still going on. When the program has finished, it will display a list of the markets that were tested and a final net profit/loss for each one. You may want to graph only one of the individual markets in the portfolio. To do that, select that market by pointing to it and clicking. The selected market will be plotted by itself, below the equity curve of the complete full portfolio.

For this first demonstration, we'll graph all the markets. Point and click on **GRAPH.** We have printed a graph that shows a 10-year equity curve of the 10-commodity portfolio, starting with $25,000 in late 1984 and growing to well over $300,000 by 1994. The equity curves of the individual commodities are plotted below. You may print this graph or return to the Main Menu. For now, return to the Main Menu by clicking on **EXIT.**

2.   Click on **CREATE REPORTS.**

You have a choice of two reports. Point and click on **SUMMARY RE-SULT REPORT,** then point and click on **VIEW.** In order to view the entire report, you must either hit the **PAGE DOWN** key or point and click on the down-pointing arrow in the lower right hand corner of the screen.

Let's go over some of the information displayed on the Summary Result Report. As you can see, the final results are based on risking $400 on each trade, and only one contract is traded for each signal during the 10-year period. Loss due to slippage and commission has been estimated at $75. (While studies have shown that this is a reasonable estimate, the program allows you to enter your own estimate for each market.)

The bottom line is an impressive $307,676 net profit for the 10-year period—a *123% average annual return for the PPS system*. PPS generated an average profit per trade of $370.69. The average winning trade was $2,194; the average loss was only $401.90. That works out to a 5.46 average win/loss ratio. Profit factor is defined as the total profit divided by the total loss; the profit factor was 2.31. All of these figures are considered very good by those in the industry who analyze systems.

Don't let the percentage of profitable trades discourage you. It is low because the money management system incorporates a close $400 stop. Often PPS is stopped out once or twice before it gets on board a profitable trend. Another statistic, maximum consecutive losses, may also be misleading. Remember, as losing trades are quickly closed with small losses, other open trades are simultaneously making profits.

Every system, even moneymakers like PPS, will have losing streaks. The maximum drawdown is a statistic based upon the most unprofitable period during the entire 10-year test. The odds of you starting to trade the system at its worst possible time are very small. With any system, the most important statistic is always how much money it made. In this test, PPS generated an average annual return of 123 percent.

When you have finished viewing this report, point and click on **EXIT.**

You are now back to the menu that allows you to select a report. This time, point and click on **DETAILED TRADE REPORT,** which will show you the trade-by-trade results during the 10-year period of the test. In order to view the entire report, you must hit the **PAGE DOWN** key or point and click on the down-pointing arrow in the lower right hand corner of the screen. When you have finished viewing this report, point and click on **EXIT.** From the Reports Menu, point and click on **DONE** to return to the Main Menu.

Customized Portfolios

The original default portfolio of 10 markets is called **start.por**. You may create other portfolios consisting of one or more markets and save them for future testing.

To create a new portfolio, place the selected commodities on the left side and click the **SAVE** icon at the bottom of the page. The message "File Save As" with the file name: start.por will appear. The cursor will be at the end of the file name. Hit either the delete key or backspace to erase this name, then type in a name for your new portfolio. All portfolio names must end with the extension .por. An example would be USJY.por as a name for a portfolio which included T-Bonds (symbol is US) and the Japanese Yen (symbol is JY).

After you have entered the new name with the .por extension, click on the **OK** key in the upper right hand corner of the window to return to a previous window that lists the selected commodities. To exit this window, click **DONE** at the bottom on the page.

When you want to retrieve this portfolio again, simply click the **LOAD** button at the bottom of the page. The next window will list all of the file names that end with the extension .por. Click to highlight the name of a portfolio, click **OK**, and the selected portfolio will be loaded. (Note: Whatever portfolio is saved to start.por will be the portfolio that is loaded when you start the program.)

Fixed-Fractional Money Management

As the account size grows, the number of contracts traded should increase. The fixed-fractional money management approach is a systematic way to equate risk to current equity; each trade's risk is a specific percent of the account size. In this demonstration disk, the risk is fixed at 2 percent of the account size. (In the full PPS Portfolio Analyzer, this is a variable controlled by the user.)

To display an equity curve with the fixed fractional approach, click on **CHANGE MONEY MANAGEMENT PARAMETERS** at the Main Menu. You will then be at the menu that allows you to change the Starting Equity and change Trade Single Contracts = (yes or no). Click on the Trade Single Contracts line. Then click the **EDIT** button. In the next window, for the New Value, type "no." Click **OK** in this window, and **OK** again in the next window to complete the setup for a fixed-fractional run. Set the **TEST PERIOD START AND STOP DATES** to 890930 and 940930, in order to view the most recent five-year period. Click on the **CREATE EQUITY CURVE GRAPH,** as you have done previously.

Compare the two graphs of the 10-commodity portfolio run over a five-year period. When only a single contract is traded per signal, the account size grows from $25,000 to more than $150,000, which is a respectable 120 percent annual return. But when the same portfolio is traded using the fixed-fractional money management approach, *the account skyrockets to $1.5 million.*

MAINTENANCE

The demonstration program restricts certain areas of the PPS Portfolio Analyzer program, but you can change the slippage and commission factor. To do so, click **MAINTENANCE**. Then highlight **CHANGE INDIVIDUAL MARKET PARAMETERS** by clicking on this line. A list of commodities will appear. Each commodity must be changed individually. Highlight one of the markets, then click **EDIT**. While there are three lines in this window, only the first line for slippage and commission can be modified in this demonstration version. Highlight **COMMISSION AND SLIPPAGE**. Click **EDIT**. In the next window, type in the new figure on the New Value line. After you have entered your new figure, click **OK**, **OK** again in the next window, and **DONE** in the last window to return to the Main Menu.

Index

Reader Services Card

Please send me information on the following:

☐ PPS Nightly Fax Service and Hotline Service

☐ PPS Seminars

☐ PPS Videos

☐ PPS Software

✂ _____

Cut or tear out and mail to:
  Curtis Arnold
  5585 Center Street
  Jupiter, FL 33458

For faster service, call (407) 747-1554 or fax this form to (407) 747-0427.

Name _____

Address _____

City/State/Zip _____

Phone (Day)_____(Evening)_____